M000190142

David Ingalls

Summer 2018
Reading for Six8 fellowship

Created in Delight

Created in Delight

Youth, Church, and the Mending of the World

TIMOTHY L. VAN METER

WIPF & STOCK · Eugene, Oregon

CREATED IN DELIGHT
Youth, Church, and the Mending of the World

Copyright © 2013 Van Meter, Timothy L.. All rights reserved. Except for
brief quotations in critical publications or reviews, no part of this book
may be reproduced in any manner without prior written permission from
the publisher. Write: Permissions, Wipf and Stock Publishers, 199 W. 8th
Ave., Suite 3, Eugene, OR 97401.

Wipf & Stock
An Imprint of Wipf and Stock Publishers
199 W. 8th Ave., Suite 3
Eugene, OR 97401
www.wipfandstock.com

ISBN 13: 978-1-61097-876-7
Manufactured in the U.S.A.

The Scripture quotations contained herein are from the New Revised
Standard Version. Bible copyright © 1989 by the Division of Christian
Education of the National Council of the Churches of Christ in the U.S.A.
Used by permission. All rights reserved.

To my father, wish you were here to challenge and celebrate and to my mother, finished the book I've been telling you about.

Contents

Acknowledgments

THIS BOOK ARISES OUT of a lifetime seeking to connect faith, hope, and love through community for the life of the world. The people who have supported my work through years of wandering toward this moment have modeled these virtues.

I wish to thank my friends and colleagues who read early drafts and offered honest feedback: Helen Blier, David White, Glenn Jordan, Chris Gardner, Julia Bingman, Mitch Kinsinger, and Greg Brown. Robin Dillon spent hours seeking the best words and order at a time when I was ready to stop, her encouragement opened the way forward. Ted Brelsford has been a colleague, friend, and now editor. I wish to thank him for his gracious copy editing.

I wish to thank my colleagues at Methodist Theological School in Ohio (MTSO) for providing both stick and carrot. I also wish to thank the great friends and colleagues at the International Association for the Study of Youth Ministry (IASYM). Their generosity in allowing me to present ideas at a formal session and then follow up for hours at a pub are models for generous and generative community.

The Youth Theological Initiative at Candler School of Theology and Leadership Now and Lancaster School of Theology were both funded through generous grants from the religion division of the Lilly Endowment. These were just two of the many Theological Programs for High School Youth that arose from the vision of Craig Dykstra and Chris Coble. These two programs offered me space for creative engagement with youth and congregations seeking theological wisdom for a sustainable world.

A little over ten years ago, a small group of young adults trusted me enough to go on retreat to Sapelo Island off the coast of

Acknowledgments

Georgia. Our time reading theology, philosophy, poetry, ecology, local history while kayaking around this barrier island continue to shape my thinking. I wish to thank Jennie A., Jennie B., J. C., Chris, Abby, Emily, Noelle, and all the other YTI alumni who came seeking a moment of peaceful insight into our complex ecological challenges.

Finally, I wish to thank Mac Browning and Chuck Foster. Mac was the best and truest example of a youth minister I will ever know, he is deeply missed by all of us who loved him. Chuck continues to be mentor, teacher, and friend. His curiosity, openness, and commitment to justice are beacons calling us all to live into true vocation.

1

Setting the Table

ON AUGUST 11, 2010, *USA Today*[1] had another article on youth ministry and how it is failing the church. It was one of many related articles in a variety of news and faith publications in the past few years. The 2008 American Religious Identification Survey (ARIS) had initiated earlier worried exchanges in both religious and secular media. This survey found that 15 percent of people in North America identified as "nones," designating no religious interest or commitment, up from 8 percent in 1990.[2] The ARIS data confirmed a 2006 Barna survey indicating that 56 percent of young people most active in church youth programs had left church altogether by ages twenty-five to thirty.[3] In Fall 2011, David Kinnaman published *You Lost Me*,[4] the latest study from Barna on young adults leaving church. Each new book and study generates more anxiety about the long-term viability of contemporary churches. Each seeks to offer reasons and responses for churches that see their influence diminishing as young people find other contexts and communities for making meaning.

1. Steinberg and Grossman, "'Forget pizza parties,' teens tell churches."
2. Kosmin et al., *American Nones.*
3. Kinnaman and Lyons, *UnChristian.*
4. Kinnaman and Hawkins, *You Lost Me.*

1

Fear and anxiety often shape conversations on adolescence and faith in media outlets and faith communities. Stories of adolescent indifference or parental irresponsibility echo and confirm the fears of anxious youth leaders, pastors, and judicatory leadership. I know these statistics are supposed drive my teaching and research, but I believe entertaining anxious echoes of fear keeps us from engaging larger questions about faith and ministry.

I believe more interesting questions can be explored, such as:

a. What are young people telling the church through their absence? The *USA Today* article had two simple answers—youth are too busy and parents are irresponsible. These easy answers allow us to avoid facing the growing irrelevance of churches for cultivating practices of lifelong faith with young people.

b. What is youth ministry? This sounds like a question with an obvious answer, but I suspect that there are as many answers as there are faith communities practicing or seeking to be in ministry with youth.

c. What kind of adults are we calling young people to be through our practices of ministry? Who in our faith communities model a compelling vision of adulthood? What is the connection between youth, healthy adulthood, and the larger world? If the institutions we currently call church were to disappear tomorrow, what could we name as communities cultivating lifelong faith?

Many young people have told me why they are leaving church and I resonate with many of their reasons. I share their frustration with a church that chooses to limit its mission through its judgments regarding who is worthy and who is unworthy of the love of God. I share their frustration with a church overly focused on those who sit in the pews on Sunday while deaf to the struggles of those outside its walls—church that allies with power while ignoring the powerless, a church that cares more about parking than the land it sits upon, more about air conditioning inside their building than air quality in their city, and more about the amount of food at a potluck than feeding the hungry. These are just a few of the frustrations that pour out when I ask young adults—"so why'd you leave?"—and am trusted enough to be offered a response beyond a shrug and a couple of syllables.

You can argue that these charges aren't fair. You can point to several examples in your church and community where this is not so. I know there are healthy places seeking resources for strengthening spaces of hope. I hope you are in the midst of building one of these places. I also hope your community is seeking its vocation as stewards of life and our planet.

John Cobb, emeritus theologian from Claremont School of Theology, calls for a renewal of faith communities by engaging the deep needs of the world. He weaves[5] a narrative of the continuing reformation of faith through the theological creativity and courage of reformers rising to challenge dead and dying religious and cultural commitments. Jesus, Augustine, Aquinas, Luther, Calvin, Wesley, Barth, Tillich, Bonhoeffer, and others live out these commitments as practices of faith for the life of the world. Cobb's prophetic call begins when faith communities engage in intentional conversation seeking the healing of the world.

Difficult conversations concerning faith and science are essential for open and healthy engagement with faith and our world. These conversations are part of the trust we hold with generations who have gone before and for generations yet to be born. Refusing to engage the big questions of our time removes the possibility of faith from people seeking to engage heart, soul and mind. Faith communities committed to seeking truth as a response to the gospel model active adult faith for young people. These communities offer the possibility for lifelong faith and a vision of spiritual maturity that will ground youth ministry and welcome the questions of young people.

The most important question framing young people today and for future generations arise out of our exploitations of the systems sustaining all life. Our ecological challenges demand our attention and creative faithful responses. Ecological youth ministry emerges

---

5. Cobb, *Spiritual Bankruptcy*.

from a desire to return in community to the texts, contexts and interpretations that have challenged and sustained faith for generations. This return offers the hopeful understanding that God may be doing a new thing in this time, in this place.

Our ecological crisis changes the landscape for how we make meaning about our place in this world and our relationships to our fellow creatures. One question shaping the future of faith communities is how we join with young people as the constructors of hope for generations yet to be born. This question is extended when we begin to understand our role in creating this mess and our vocation in constructing resilient responses for all creatures to thrive. Can we think of our faith communities as spaces that incubate hope for the decades of work that stewardship requires? Can we build spaces for celebrating abundance in resistance to declarations of scarcity that our economic, political, and cultural systems support? Scarcity seeks to filter limited resources to fewer and fewer people in support of power and wealth. Lives grounded in abundance seek to make sure that everyone has enough, not just for survival but for the celebration of jubilee.

Because we don't perceive any problem, or possibly due to willful ignorance, our commitments to consumption and comfort are diminishing the capacity for our children, grandchildren, and future generations to thrive. The short-term reward is relative comfort and repressing our growing anxiety that all might not be as we imagine it to be. The church contributes to this blindness when it constructs theologies that diminish our vocation as stewards of creation. The church's commitment to young people to live with them in truth begins in seeking understanding, in constructing theologies that seek God's life-giving vision for God's good world.

New York Times' chief science reporter, Andrew Revkin, starkly stated our shared future in an interview in late November, 2008. Revkin was asked if climate change was the most important story of our day. He replied that the challenges facing us have evolved and climate change was just one of many challenges facing the planet and human thriving: "Climate change is a subset of the story of our time, which is that we are coming of age on a finite planet and only just now recognizing that it is finite. So how we mesh infinite aspirations of a species that's been on this explosive trajectory—not just of population growth but of consumptive appetite—how can we make a transition to a sort of stabilized and still prosperous relationship with the Earth and each other is the story of our time."[6]

The recognition of limits and the discipline of our appetites are aspects of ancient, and perhaps archaic, virtues of the Christian faith. The Western cultural construction of Christianity has difficulty cultivating these virtues. However, rather than proceeding with an ecologically destructive theological/atheological construction of adolescence that offers insights such as "you can become anything you desire, just work hard enough," or other aphorisms supporting a theology of Western exceptionalism, it is time to call theological foundations of youth ministry as it is practiced to a sustainable hermeneutic. Revkin continues with an even more sobering assessment:

> And it's a story about conflict. It's a story about the fact that there are a billion teenagers on planet earth right now. A hundred thirty years ago there were only a billion people altogether—grandparents, kids. Now there are a billion teenagers and they could just as easily become child soldiers and drug dealers as innovators and the owners of small companies in favelas in Brazil. And little tweaks in their prospects, a little bit of education, a little bit of opportunity, a micro loan or something, something that gets girls into schools, those things—that's the story of our time. And climate change is like a symptom of the story of our time, meaning our energy choices right now come with a lot of emissions of greenhouse gases and if we don't have a lot of new [choices] we're going to have a lot of warming.[7]

Revkin articulates the unavoidable realization that we live in a finite system. The earth has limits to the amount of resources and energy we can extract. Though there is a significant amount of new energy entering the earth every day, it isn't entering as oil or coal; these are the products of ancient sunlight that we mine for contemporary

6. Revkin, "Climate, 'Not the Story of Our Time.'"
7. Ibid.

use. He is also clear that the generation to bear the cost of terrestrial limits is with us. There are now a billion teenagers living on the planet, many of them in poverty, in the midst of conflict and scrambling at the edges of economic and political life. We are consuming the good things of the world at the expense of our children.

Paolo Bacigalupi, a science-fiction writer, offers a striking metaphor to which I'll refer throughout this book. He writes,

> Whenever I think about the environment (Be Green; Love Mother Earth; Blah Blah Blah), I like to think of a family going out to a nice restaurant. Mom and Dad place their orders—but for some reason, the kids don't get anything. Instead, the kids wait and watch while their parents gobble down dinner.
>
> Their parents eat the arugula salad, the rosemary-infused bread, the sun-dried tomato farfalle, the veal piccata, and generally have a pretty great time. Maybe Mom's wearing pearls, because, you know, it's a nice restaurant. Dad is definitely wearing a tie—he's classy that way. Mom and Dad go through a couple bottles of wine, linger over the tiramisu, and then, when they're stuffed to the gills, they shove their picked-over and scraped-over plates down the table to their children, with the last bits of pasta and the runny lines of sauce, and some chewed-up bits of meat, and say, "Here kids, eat up!"
>
> So the kids get the scraps, while their parents get the meal.
>
> And then, to top it all off, Mom and Dad get up from the table and walk out the door, leaving the kids to deal with the pissed-off waiter who just showed up saying that the credit card has been declined. So the kids end up washing dishes in the back for the next couple hundred years to pay off the bill.
>
> That's Environment 101. The first person at the table gets the cheap energy, the clean water, the clean air, the rain forests, the coral reefs, and the open space, and has all the fun. The last person gets stuck with the cleanup and the bill. The last person is always going to be a kid. It's not personal. It's just the way things work out.[8]

8. Scalzi, "The Big Idea—Paulo Bacigalupi."

I sometimes hear from faithful people the comment that our kids are so talented and so connected to nature that they will have no problem cleaning up the mess we made. This sounds like idle chatter from the adults at Bacigalupi's dinner. "Yes, yes, the kids will clean it up, we may have overspent a bit, maybe we tore up a few things, maybe we even indulged beyond our means, don't worry young people are more than capable of taking care of it."

Youth ministry that imitates the larger consumptive culture, rather than seeking healing and transformation, denies the goodness of God's creation. Stewardship begins by knowing our limits and joining with God in the naming and transformation of this earth into God's kin-dom[9] for all creatures.

We are living in the midst of radical change to the life sustaining systems of our planet. Our young people are inheriting an ecological mess. They will need to discover and cultivate resources for redefining their lives in cooperation with life on this planet. I understand that to seek to be faithful is to choose to be constrained by hope. Despair isn't merely a luxury but anti-gospel. Faith that takes seriously the thriving of all life—and not just human life—is an essential resource for this generation and generations to follow. The church has resources introducing youth and young adults to the struggles for meaning of generations who have gone before as well as opening possibilities for generations yet to be born. This book is one small attempt to open up those possibilities. I hope it invites curiosity and renewed practices for sustaining and sustainable faith.

The practices of youth and young adult ministry on a planet with recognized limits can't support the greed of any generation, but seeks to cultivate practices enhancing life and health for all generations. Those of us who understand ourselves to be called into ministry for, by, and with young people should be seeking ways to stand with them in engaging these limits. It is incumbent on

9. While "kingdom" is often used as a metaphor for the reign of God, the theological voices underlying this work privilege relational language, such as kin-dom rather than language that reinforces the power structures that can give permission unchecked exploitation, e.g., the king has the power to take what he wants, when we live with kin we seek ways for all to thrive.

faithful people that we seek ways to live into creation's abundance, offering a place for all, but to resist seductions of greed, objectification of God's goodness, and mindless growth limiting the futures of generations to come. Our world has finite resources and finite capacity for absorbing the impact of human activity. With the largest human population in the history of the world, over a billion of which are teenagers, is this beginning to sound like a concern for youth ministry?

ABOUT THIS BOOK

The first question for any church seeking to be involved in youth and young adult ministry has to be "how might we offer ourselves to the lives of young people?" Unfortunately, the initial question too often is "how might we attract, persuade, control, or capture youth for the future of our institution?"

Youth and/or young adult ministry can be frustrating. Too often we are mindful of the next challenge, the next program, the latest problem brought by pastor, parent, or adolescent. Youth ministry framed by our fear, incuriosity, or incompetence can truncate any understanding of the gospel. I proved this observation true in my first stint in youth ministry in the 1970s and 1980s. Primarily unaware of my own anxiety and entanglements, I became a booster of easy, unthinking assent to simplistic, formulaic beliefs.

This book is first and foremost meant to challenge and support those who minister with youth and young adults to consider ministry through an ecological lens. Not at the expense of a biblical, theological, ecclesial, or even eschatological lens, but because the deep needs of our time require we do so.

This book is written with three audiences in mind. The first are youth workers. I hope to support those who are already asking ecological questions in their ministry. The second are future leaders of churches who won't have the luxury of anxiously looking back to the glory days of dying institutions. The students I have the privilege of teaching are more comfortable with the end of Christendom and are excited by the possibilities of leading faith communities less enamored with being at the center of power.

Third, I want to challenge those trying to ignore our ecological reality and using the language of faith to denigrate science. I support the idea that beliefs are important for structuring our lives but science has different epistemological commitments; it isn't merely belief. Physics, chemistry, biology, and the interaction of the earth's systems don't much care what your beliefs might be. Faith seeks understanding and meaning through our experiences and the experiences of faithful ancestors living in conversation with texts, practices, rituals, symbols, etc. The sciences are grounded in seeking a plausible hypothesis for observable phenomena, testing that hypothesis for its viability in explaining the phenomena, and in time and with repeated gathering of support and evidence, in building a foundation for understanding our world.

Faith approaches questions differently than science. Faith is about making meaning with different ways of discovery and knowing. Science and faith give us two different languages and modes for understanding. Sometimes these two languages can be in harmony with one another; in other ways they may be discordant, but facility with both languages is essential.

This book follows my own journey toward an ecological hermeneutic for youth ministry. Core questions about youth and young adult ministry have framed my entire vocational life. How do practices that allow space for both faith and doubt open possibilities for ministry? Who are we calling young people to become? How do our relationships with young people call us to deeper understanding of our own formation? How is our sense of vocation changed when we understand ourselves as creatures in relationship with our fellow creatures in the midst of creation? What are the practices of stewardship that allow us to live more fully into our lives in vocation? How do we begin to think of our lives as hopeful companions with God's work in the healing of the world? What does it mean to be faithful as a people seeking to live in God's created abundance, rather than consumers chasing illusions of greed in the midst of scarcity? How do we construct resilient communities of grace?

I hope this book will play a part in cultivating hope in the midst of rapid and possibly catastrophic changes. I realize if I want to hold credibility with certain people of faith I should probably say "if" there is great change or "if" the possible ecological stresses come to be. But it's too late for "if." We have already reshaped our world beyond "if." We have to seek hope in the midst of an ever more troubling now. There is little good news, but to be a person of faith, particularly a person who follows Christ, is to be constrained by hope. Despair is not an option.

The attempt to paint Christianity 'green' as it is commonly understood and practiced in North America is a fool's pursuit. We function in North America as consumers of faith, just as we are consumers of everything else. There is absolutely no point in greening a faith that facilitates our narcissism. The gospel of Jesus Christ and the health of the world would be best served if we shut up, slowed down, and sought God by embracing our vocation as stewards and partnering with God for the health of all creation. This book attempts to explore how we might do this in our relationships with youth, young adults, and the more than human world.

Sustaining Practices

I conclude the rest of the chapters with short questions, practices, etc. For this chapter do a brief reflection on your connection to the topic of the book and the communities available for you to engage these questions more deeply. The pattern is:

For the Reader—

Additional resources/practices to ground the reader in the theme of the chapter.

For your Youth—

Questions/resources/practices opening the reader to listening to young people and inviting young people into the conversation.

For your Faith Community—

Seeking places for young people and adults to join together in action/practice/learning.

2

Ecological Disconsolations

IN 2005, I TRAVELED to northern India with friends. On the flight from New Delhi to Ladakh, I pressed my face up against the airplane window and watched the mountains grow from foothills to the massive Himalayas. They had features I knew from other mountain ranges, but the scale blew my mind. The Himalayas dwarfed the Rockies, the Alps, or the Cascades, let alone the Appalachians. I was awestruck by their enormity. Then the remnants of my old geological training began to kick in. How are they formed? The rock doesn't look igneous, could it be sedimentary? I couldn't wait to land for a closer examination.

Through the plane's window, I saw the u-shaped valleys and rock formations that indicated significant glacial activity. The terminal moraines (rock piled up at the lower end of a glacier) held back lakes of bluish green water, far below the glacial ice higher up the side of the mountain. These lakes contained water from the seasonal ice and glaciers melting above them. The moraines and their lakes appeared to be miles from their source and I wondered if the glaciers might be in retreat. Our plane landed and we began to explore the area. By explore I mean moving thirty meters from the tent to the dining area or another fifteen meters to the Indus river, our bodies struggling to acclimate to our camp at eleven thousand feet.

The following day, we joined a young Buddhist monk on a tour of local monasteries. After a couple of hours he asked if we had noticed the Indus River. It was impossible to ignore the fast-flowing bluish-green water and so we answered half-joking, "Yes, the river was comforting us as we tried to learn to breathe again."

The monk continued, "The water in the Indus is essential for our neighbors in Pakistan. If this river dies, when the glaciers are gone, we will certainly go to war." The Indus River flows out of Tibet, through northern India into Pakistan. The retreating glaciers I observed as we flew into Ladakh were the source of water sustaining life in Pakistan, or if they flowed into the Ganges, then in India. I asked our guide what he thought of global warming. "No doubt, it is happening, I am watching it. But like many things unnoticed in the West, the poor will bear the price."

This wasn't my first time to see glaciers. As an undergraduate geology major, my summer field course was a four-week trip up the spine of the Rockies, learning alpine geomorphology with an emphasis on the role of glaciers. It was a brilliant time, paying attention to mountain features I'd overlooked on previous trips as a winter skier and summer backpacker. We hiked up to a hanging glacier in Rocky Mountain National Park in Colorado, hiked in the Tetons and Wind River mountains in Wyoming. We spent four days in Glacier National Park in Montana exploring the impact of ice on the alpine environment. We concluded our study at the Athabaska glacier in the Columbia ice field in Jasper National Park in western Canada, clambering on the edge of the ice, carefully avoiding the crevasses. It was more a traveling seminar than a research-based course, but I appreciated the opportunity for learning in the field.

This undergraduate course was a significant moment in my vocational discernment. I learned a lot about necessary qualities for a geologist and I learned that at that time in my life I didn't have them. I lacked the patience necessary for close observation, for gathering and cataloguing discrete bits of data, and the endurance to go out every day for years building knowledge of place and geological processes that could eventually reveal significant insights. The field course deepened my respect for scientists who patiently observe, record, and interpret data. It was just a couple of years after earning a bachelor's degree in geology that I returned to youth ministry, this time as a professional.

Neither a travel anecdote nor a degree in geology credentials me as an environmental expert. However, this background along with my life-long love for creation has led me to look more deeply into the work of real climate scientists as well as the work of those engaging other environmental challenges. I ask you to join me both in close observation and in cultivating a deeper love for the world we inhabit. This chapter is a brief exploration of the observations and conclusions of scientists working on climate change and other ecological sciences. You might begin with what I've gathered here, but your investigation must extend well beyond the scope of this book. Understanding science and some ability to engage in thoughtful dialogue around scientific hypotheses, theories, and observations are necessary practices for people involved in ministering to young people because these are primary practices of human meaning making.[1]

OUR ECOLOGICAL CONTEXT

Rather than observing the glaciers in India, I could have flown over the Rockies and wondered how water would be distributed for the next century from the Colorado River in the western United States. Or I could have visited the Columbia ice fields in Canada again and walked on bare ground covered by thirty feet of ice on my first visit in 1984 or even my last visit in 1995. Or I could have sat on a bench overlooking the Mississippi river in 2011 and watched the record floods, thinking about the heavy snows and hard rains producing the third five-hundred-year flood in fifty years.

While glaciers melt in one part of the world and floods grow in frequency and scope in other parts of the world, other areas are

---

1. Subscribe to *Science, Scientific American,* or *Nature* magazines or subscribe to their free daily updates in your email. If this sounds like too much, sit down with a science teacher in your local middle school or high school and ask how you can support them as they explore ideas in biology, chemistry, or physics with youth. Learn about evolutionary biology, new discoveries in astronomy, study the life of a local pond—learn the world, as best you can through the eyes of a scientist. You may never know as much as your local high school teacher, or your shared students, but you will begin to cultivate new ways of seeing, learning, and loving our world.

in the midst of record droughts. In July 2012, the US Department of Agriculture declared a drought emergency. As the summer continues, more counties were added to the emergency declaration, allowing the USDA to offer assistance to farmers and ranchers throughout the US. By August 29, the US Department of Agriculture had "designated 1,892 unduplicated counties in 38 states as disaster areas—1,820 due to drought."[2] 2012 over 60 percent of the continental United States was experiencing drought conditions. This could affect food prices and availability for 2013.[3] The weather the continental United States has experienced the first half of 2012 is consistent with the troubling scenarios climate scientists have been warning us about for over twenty years.

The twelve-month period from June 2011 through June 2012 is the hottest on record.[4] We live in a world in which global greenhouse gas emissions hit record highs each successive year and small island nations in the south Pacific like Tuvalu and Nauru are slowly disappearing under the rising seas. It's a world where monsoons in Bangladesh and India cause greater casualties and cover more land as oceans rise and storms bear more precipitation. We watch floods in the Mississippi and Ohio valleys strip diminishing topsoil every year, forcing farmers to use more fertilizer to increase crop yields. Runoffs from these fields contain high levels of nitrogen and other nutrients that produce hypoxic (dead) zones in the Gulf of Mexico.

In 1988 James Hansen, a NASA climatologist, testified before Congress that they were beginning to see the effects of global warming on climate. *The New York Times* reported his testimony was received with concern and a call to action by a number of senators present at the hearing: "'Global warming has reached a level such that we can ascribe with a high degree of confidence a cause and effect relationship between the greenhouse effect and observed warming,' Dr. Hansen said at the hearing today, adding, 'It

2. USDA News Release No. 0284.12.

3. Baker, "Drought Puts Food at Risk, US Warns," A17.

4. Interactive tools are available on the NOAA website that allows the user to plot temperature data. This particular tool is found at http://www.ncdc. noaa.gov/temp-and-precip/time-series/index.php?parameter=tmp&month= 6&year=2012&filter=12&state=110&div=0.

is already happening now."[5] Twenty years later, Dr. Hansen warned that we need to cap our atmospheric CO_2 at 350 ppm if we want to maintain a climate allowing human civilization to flourish.[6] The National Oceanic and Atmospheric Administration (NOAA) found that the average mean surface measurement of CO_2 for 2010 was 390.11. The mean average for 2011 was 392.09. This measurement has been rising since continuous monitoring began in 1958.[7] On May 31, 2012, the NOAA released a news story stating that several monitoring stations had found that 400 ppm of atmospheric CO_2 was measured in the Arctic. A NOAA news release dated May 31, 2012 quotes atmospheric scientist Pieter Tans, "The northern sites in our monitoring network tell us what is coming soon to the globe as a whole . . . We will likely see global average CO_2 concentrations reach 400 ppm about 2016."[8]

In *Eaarth*, Bill McKibben relates a story detailing the frustration and fear gripping scientists as they try to relate their observations. "In the summer of 2008, at an academic conference at Britain's Exeter University, a scientist named Kevin Anderson took the podium for a major address. He showed slide after slide, graph after graph, 'representing the fumes that belch from chimneys, exhausts and jet engines, that should have bent in a rapid curve towards the ground, were heading for the ceiling instead.' His conclusion: it was 'improbable' that we'd be able to stop short of 650 parts per million (of CO_2 in the atmosphere), even if rich countries adopted draconian emissions reductions within a decade."[9]

In 2007, the Intergovernmental Panel on Climate Change (IPCC) released a series of reports detailing a conservative overview of current findings concerning climate change. The executive summary begins with the statement that "[W]arming of the climate system is unequivocal, as is now evident from observations of increases in global average air and ocean temperatures, widespread

5. Shabecoff, "Global Warming has Begun."

6. Hansen, "Target Atmospheric CO_2," 1.

7. http://www.esrl.noaa.gov/gmd/. All data for this paragraph is from the NOAA website.

8. NOAA, "Carbon Dioxide," para. 4.

9. McKibben, *Eaarth*, 18.

melting of snow and ice and rising global average sea level."[10] The IPCC reports summarize hundreds of scientific studies concluding that while scientific research continues to understand the extent of human contributions to climate change, it is a matter of *how much*, not *if* human beings are changing the world's climate. The executive summary ends with a warning: "Key vulnerabilities may be associated with many climate-sensitive systems, including food supply, infrastructure, health, water resources, coastal systems, ecosystems, global biogeochemical cycles, ice sheets and modes of oceanic and atmospheric circulation."[11]

Each day brings another dire assessment of the extent of environmental damage and the increasing rate of decline. In October 2009, the IPCC released a revision of its earlier report under the headline "World is committed to 1.8 to 4.9 degrees Celsius of warming even if action were immediate."[12] On June 16, 2009, the US Global Change Research Program issued a report titled *Global Change Impacts in the United States*. More than fifty scientists and policy makers from thirteen government agencies participated as authors and signatories to the final report. The executive summary begins:

> Observations show that the warming of the climate is unequivocal. The global warming observed over the past 50 years is due primarily to human-induced emissions and heat-trapping gases. These emissions come primarily from the burning of fossil fuels (coal, oil and gas) with important contributions from the clearing of forests, agricultural practices, and other activities.
>
> Warming over this century is projected to be considerably greater than over the last century. The global average temperature since 1900 has risen by about 1.5°F. By 2100, it is projected to rise another 2 to 11.5°F. The US average temperature has risen a comparable amount and is very likely to rise more than the global average over this century.[13]

10. IPCC, *Climate Change* 2007, 30.
11. Ibid., 18.
12. Jowit, "World's Glaciers Continue to Melt at Historic Rates," 14.
13. Karl, "Global Change Impacts in the United States," 3.

Immediately after its release, this report was reviewed and referenced in several publications and websites. The reviews ranged from panicked and dire "I told you so" to "well I guess I'll get used to milder winters," though the idea of a milder winter might be a bit optimistic in referencing a report that says Kansas can expect one hundred eighty days a year over 90°F, with summertime highs from 110° to 118°F while the deep south and most of the southwest are projected to remain in perpetual drought.

In June 2011, the National Climate Data Center, a department in the NOAA and the US Department of Commerce released a report on the State of the Climate 2010.[14] It was compiled from the contributions of over three hundred fifty scientists from forty-eight different countries studying climate change around the world. The report concurred that 2010 was one of the two hottest years on record, sea levels continue to rise, and ice at the poles continues to melt. The ice melt in the Arctic was so extensive that both the Northwest Passage and the Northern Sea route were open for navigation for the first time in recorded history.

Earlier that same June, the International Program on the State of the Ocean held a conference that brought together a diverse group of marine scientists. "The workshop enabled leading experts to take a global view on how all the different effects we are having on the ocean are compromising its ability to support us. This examination of synergistic threats leads to the conclusion that we have underestimated the overall risks and that the whole of marine degradation is greater than the sum of its parts, and that degradation is now happening at a faster rate than predicted." [15]

They released a summary of their findings on June 21, 2011. The summary listed the key points of concern:

- Human actions have resulted in warming and acidification of the oceans and are now causing increased hypoxia.

- The speeds of many negative changes to the ocean are near to or are tracking the worst case scenarios from IPCC and other predictions.

14. Blunden, "State of the Climate."
15. Rogers, "Ocean Stresses," 5.

- These 'worst case' effects are compounding other changes more consistent with predictions including: changes in the distribution and abundance of marine species; changes in primary production; changes in the distribution of harmful algal blooms; increases in health hazards in the oceans; and loss of large, long-lived fish species causing the simplification and destabilization of food webs in marine ecosystems.

- The magnitude of the cumulative impacts on the ocean is greater than previously understood.

- Our time for action addressing these problems is shrinking and the resources available for creating healthy solutions are diminishing. The longer we wait the higher the associated costs and the poorer the possibilities for success.

- Resilience of the oceans to climate change impacts is severely compromised by the other stressors from human activities, including fisheries, pollution, and habitat destruction.

- Ecosystem collapse is occurring as a result of both current and emergent stressors.

- The extinction threat to marine species is rapidly increasing.[16]

At the end of this list of ocean stresses, the program participants "concluded that not only are we already experiencing severe declines in many species to the point of commercial extinction in some cases, and an unparalleled rate of regional extinctions of habitat types (e.g., mangroves and seagrass meadows), but we now face losing marine species and entire marine ecosystems, such as coral reefs, within a single generation. Unless action is taken now, the consequences of our activities are at a high risk of causing, through the combined effects of climate change, overexploitation, pollution and habitat loss, the next globally significant extinction event in the ocean."[17]

To read the entire report, or to read the earlier referenced reports, or to read the reports that will be generated by groups of scientists from the time I wrote this chapter until the moment you

16. Ibid., 5–6.
17. Ibid., 7.

read it, will deepen despair and do little to cultivate hope. So what can we do? How do we even begin to engage these problems? All environmental trends appear to be moving toward a worsening climate, poorer soils, critically ill oceans, ever-diminishing biodiversity, compromised resilience in natural systems, and less time to respond to build health.

WHY DON'T WE SEE?

The science is dire. Scientists, artists, naturalists, and environmentally aware citizens of all nations consistently remind us of the necessity of immediate action. Yet, policy makers, news media, and—at least in the United States—our daily lives continue without regard to the growing crisis. Why don't we perceive our diminishing resources? Does our relative comfort today blind our thoughts of tomorrow? Our comfort today is at the expense of generations to follow. I suspect they will have many words and phrases for our blind narcissism.

We begin by paying attention. Ed Ayres, former director of the Worldwatch Institute, articulated the necessity of shifting our awareness of ecological challenges in *God's Last Offer*. He warns that it's difficult, nearly impossible to perceive things that lie outside of all previous experience. A substantive shift in the life sustaining systems of the earth fits the category of the inconceivable. Ayres identifies several factors that contribute to our inability to perceive and respond. These include, first of all, intentional misinformation campaigns by industrial, political, and economic groups that seek to minimize awareness of human impact on the environment and to limit the debate on sustainable models of industrial and economic development.

Bill McKibben clarifies why energy companies pour millions of dollars into denial and delaying tactics. He says, "in ecological terms it would be extremely prudent to write off $20 trillion of [petroleum] reserves. In economic terms, of course, it would be a disaster, first and foremost for shareholders and executives from companies like ExxonMobil. If you run an oil company, this sort of write-off is the disastrous future staring you in the face as soon as climate change is taken as seriously as it should be . . . It's why you'll do anything—including fund an endless campaign of lies—to avoid coming to terms with its reality."[18]

A second difficulty in framing and understanding our contemporary ecological crisis is the constantly changing and growing body of information throughout our entire culture. The pace of discovery, the generation of new information, and the speed of change challenges our ability to understand the scope and depth of a problem. The information tsunami we live through each day keeps us always ingesting new information and constrains the ability to reflect on what we know. We live feeling that we never have enough information to analyze and respond adequately to any problems, so we rarely turn off the fire hose in order to assess and respond. Crises become worse when we only react; we need times to pause, reflect, and construct new ways of engaging problems that allow all life to thrive.

The earlier referenced 2009 report, *Global Change Impacts in the United States*, is an attempt to plan for the impact of climate change in seven broad categories: water resources, energy supply and use, transportation, agriculture, ecosystems, human health, and society. Each category interacts with the others and has an impact on the severity of the impact of the other challenges. Think again about the five-hundred-year floods in the Mississippi valley. The flooded river affected cities' water supplies, human health, the destruction of roads, and chemicals flushed into the Gulf of Mexico changing the balance hundreds of miles downstream.

A third factor affecting our ability to perceive the scope of our contemporary environmental challenge emerges from our faith in human ingenuity to cope with any problems and/or our trust in divine intervention to save us from the consequences of our own actions. Environmental destruction arising out of the historical alliance between capitalism and Christianity is the thesis of Lynn White's 1967 essay "The Historical Roots of the Environmental Crisis." The connection between our commitment to technocratic scientific understandings and the dominant Western Christian

18. McKibben, "Why the Energy-Industry Elite Has It In for the Planet."

view of exploiting the world bear some of the blame for our continued inability to perceive our immersion in ecologically destructive lifestyles.

Finally, we are blinded by the inability to think holistically about local or global ecological problems due to increased specialization. The scientists at the 2011 Oceans Conference are an example of how knowledge is discovered through commitment to discrete disciplines. The interdisciplinary conversations they held at that conference focused their need for immediate action. They speak of the imminent collapse of ocean eco-systems. As some of the top people in their individual fields, they understood how systems they studied were under stress. It was only at a conference (I suspect as much at the dinner table as at any paper presentation) that they discovered the dire state of the oceans.

Each of these aspects allows for our collective blindness, and each of them can be made worse through unthinking religious commitments. We can remain convinced that God will save us through our theologies of escape or we can believe that our ingenuity will save us through new technologies allowing us to continue to consume without consequences. The first is an eschatological position that allows human beings to consume our world because we believe it is less than God's good creation. At its worst this belief system offers rescue at the end of our exploitation.

A second belief system gives us permission to consume millions of years of energy stored as carbon based fuels arising from faith in our own ingenuity and technological prowess. A belief that we will invent new ways to reduce waste, use energy, and maintain our comfort is a belief in an imaginary technological utopia. Both of these misguided belief systems continue practices of exploitation and planetary degradation diminishing the lives of generations today and for decades in the future.

The warnings of the past few decades are now observable reality. James Hansen and other climate change researchers are becoming more vocal about the destructive path our political and economic commitments are blazing. In February 2012, Hansen presented his concerns at a February TED conference.[19] Hansen

19. Hansen, "Why I Must Speak Out About Climate Change."

reviewed his career in climate science and paused to reflect on how he will answer his grandchildren when they ask if he's done all he could. Hansen's review of the science underlying global warming is followed by a brief overview of heatwaves, droughts, hurricanes, and other large weather events occurring around the world. Hansen continues, "(f)ifty years ago, such anomalies covered only two- to three-tenths of one percent of the land area. In recent years, because of global warming, they now cover about 10 percent—an increase by a factor of 25 to 50."[20]

Have we done enough? Are we doing enough? No, if James Hansen grieves for his grandchildren and worries that he hasn't done all he could, then I am certain that I haven't even begun to do enough.

We are approaching the limits of our planet's ability to sustain the resource rich lifestyle we believe to be our birthright. We need to return to the sources offering meaning and hope and construct new visions for vocation grounding our relationship to our world and our fellow creatures in structures allowing our mutual thriving.

Sustaining Practices

For the Reader—

Read Bill McKibben's *Eaarth* as a way to begin to understand the challenge of climate change. Begin to gather all the information you can to understand climate change and our ecological challenges.

For your Youth—

Gather a small group of young people, ask what concerns them when they think of their future and the world's future.

For your Faith Community—

Gather a group to study and discuss your faith tradition's/denomination's statement on climate change.

20. Ibid.

3

On Earth as in Heaven

DRIVEN TO DESPAIR

I HAVE BEEN READING and thinking about ecological issues for almost thirty years and find the growing body of data dense and difficult to digest. There is so little good news and so much bad news as we continue to outline our growing global ecological challenges. On most days I want to flee as far as possible from my earlier charge to 'pay attention!' Why would anyone want to pay attention when each new piece of information adds to a sense of helplessness?

Scott Russell Sanders is an essayist who seeks to cultivate hope in the midst of our new reality. In *Hunting for Hope*, he explores a larger vision of living more deeply into our contexts and relationships as he seeks to reconnect with his teenage son. A backpacking trip in the Rocky Mountains begins well and then deteriorates. By the end of the first day, father and son are muttering under their breath, unable to understand why they decided to hike together, as well as questioning how they could be possibly be related to each other.

On a drive away from the trailhead, Sanders returns to his son's last jab,

'So what are my hang-ups?' I demanded. 'How do I ruin everything?'

'You don't want to know,' he said.

'I want to know. What is it about me that grates on you?'

I do not pretend to recall the exact words we hurled at one another after my challenge, but I remember the tone and thrust of them, and here is how they have stayed with me:

'You wouldn't understand,' he said.

'Try me.'

He cut a look at me, shrugged, then stared back through the windshield. 'You're just so out of touch.'[1]

Sanders details the fragmented relationship he was seeking to mend. He and his son trade barbs as Sanders aptly portrays the miscommunication that can only come in relationship with those we love. He's out of touch, he hates everything his son loves, he hates the world his son is growing up in and his generation built. Sander's son echoes a litany of frustration and despair felt by many youth and young adults.

'You look at any car and all you think is pollution, traffic, roadside crap. You say fast food's poisoning our bodies and TV's poisoning our minds. You think the internet is just another scam for selling stuff. You think business is a conspiracy to rape the earth.'

'None of that bothers you?'

'Of course it does. But that's the world. That's where we've got to live. It's not going to go away just because you don't approve. What's the good of spitting on it?'

'I don't spit on it. I grieve over it.'

He was still for a moment, then resumed quietly. 'What's the good of grieving if you can't change anything?'

'Who says you can't change anything?'

'You do. Maybe not with your mouth, but with your eyes.' Jesse rubbed his own eyes, and the words came out muffled through his cupped palms. 'Your view of things is totally dark. It bums me out. You make me feel as if the

1. Sanders, *Hunting for Hope*, 8.

planet's dying and people are to blame and nothing can be done about it. There's no room for hope. Maybe you can get by without hope, but I can't. I've got a lot of living still to do. I have to believe there's a way we can get out of this mess. Otherwise what's the point? Why study, why work–why do anything if it's all going to hell?'

That sounded unfair to me, a caricature of my views, and I thought of many sharp replies; yet there was too much truth and too much hurt in what he said for me to fire back an answer. Had I really deprived my son of hope? Was this the deeper grievance—that I had passed on to him, so young, my anguish over the world? Was this what lurked between us, driving us apart, the demon called despair?

'You're right,' I finally told him. 'Life's meaningless without hope. But I think you're wrong to say I've given up.'

'It seems that way to me. As if you think we're doomed.'

'No buddy. I don't think we're doomed. It's just that nearly everything I care about is under assault.'

'See that's what I mean. You're so worried about the fate of the earth, you can't enjoy anything. We come to these mountains and you bring the shadows with you. You've got me seeing nothing but darkness.'

Stunned by the force of his words, I could not speak. If my gloom cast a shadow over Creation for my son, then I had failed him. What remedy could there be for such a betrayal?[2]

Sanders's dialogue with his son causes me to wonder how often I've done this. Lost in my own despair, how often have I been the one to kill hope for young people? Our ecological outlook is increasingly dire. But if all I can do is articulate despair without cultivating hope, then this is a fresh betrayal. To be a follower of Christ is to choose to be constrained by hope. This hope is neither facile nor naïve. We often confuse the hard work of hope with the foolishness of unthinking optimism. To choose to walk with young people is to become cultivators of hope for this generation and generations

2. Ibid., 8–10.

to come. If we can only articulate despair, trapped in anger at the destruction we as a species are committing, then we have betrayed young people and our vocation.

How do we find a path of hope in the midst of all we are discovering? It's the challenge of our age. We have to push ourselves back from Bacigalupi's banquet table and invite young people to a different place of abundance: one in which they not only have a share, but where they are building a larger vision for the generations that will follow.

In 2004, biologist E. O. Wilson wrote *The Creation,* a book written as a letter to an imagined conservative Christian minister asking for a dialogue to address our shared experience on this planet. Wilson has studied how climate change, species degradation, the loss of habitat, and other environmental challenges are altering the very systems that sustain all of life. Wilson seeks common commitments, opening dialogue, and partnership. One avenue to such dialogue and partnership is our sense of connection to the incredible gift of our shared context. Wilson's invitation to partnership doesn't require a shared understanding of the origination of life, merely the recognition that the world we inhabit is perfectly suited for life to thrive. We have decisions to make about how we will cultivate this thriving or whether we will choose to exploit it. Whether we understand this place we live as God's creation or as the result of millions of years of evolution, we can agree that we live in a world for which we are perfectly suited.

Wilson asks that we join in preserving the life of the world, since the life of the world preserves us all.

> Our relationship to Nature is primal. The emotions it evokes arose during the forgotten prehistory of mankind [*sic*] and hence are deep and shadowed. Like childhood experiences lost from conscious memory, they are commonly felt but rarely articulated. Poets, at the highest level of human expression, try. They know something fundamental moves beneath the surface of our conscious minds, something worth saving. It evokes some of the spirituality that you and I, Pastor, hold in common." . . .
> (T)he gravitational pull of Nature on the human psyche

can be expressed in a single, more contemporary expression, biophilia, which I defined in 1984 as the innate tendency to affiliate with life and lifelike processes."[3]

Wilson's invitation to cultivate biophilia is a request for peace in a longer skirmish. Biophilia underlies our attraction to the pets that enrich our lives, the desire to view animals in the wild, and all those ways we fulfill our desire to be in relationship with other creatures.

Almost forty years earlier, UCLA Professor of History (and United Church of Christ layperson) Lynn White Jr. published a short article entitled "The Historical Roots of the Environmental Crisis" in the journal *Science*. White believed real environmental health was impossible due to an alliance between Christianity and capitalism. This destructive relationship at the root of Western culture inevitably leads to the degradation of the environment. White calls Christianity "the most anthropocentric religion the world has seen."[4] Christianity "not only established a dualism of man [*sic*] and nature but also insisted that it is God's will that man exploit nature for his proper ends."[5] Christian thinkers and theologians have thoughtfully engaged White's critique and offered alternative understandings of the Christian view of the human relationship with nature and fellow creatures. Some appear in this work and many more have shaped my thinking.[6]

I concede that cultural practices driving us to this desperate point in our history are deeply entwined with our theologies. The biblical creation narratives speak of human beings as stewards of the abundance in partnership as members of God's good creation. However, our culture of extraction and consumption has shaped

3. Wilson, *Creation*, 63.

4. White, "Roots," 1967.

5. Ibid.

6. H. Paul Santmire, John Cobb, Sallie McFague, Douglas John Hall and many other theologians have unpacked White's simplistic argument and construct a much richer understanding of the relationships between Christianity, capitalism, and the environment. However, Lynn White's critique is worth reading both for its continuing impact and as a brief overview of how Christianity is often seen as the source of ecological problems rather than partners in healing.

our theology, replacing stewardship with domination, abundance with scarcity, and hospitality with anxiety.

The ecological crisis changes the landscape for faith and creaturely thriving. The last few decades of exploitation have allowed people of faith to confuse greed with blessing. Discovering the limits of our planet to support our greed will raise new questions for faith communities. Can we, as people of faith, think of our faith communities as spaces that incubate hope? Can we build spaces for celebrating abundance in resistance to a culture of scarcity? A culture of scarcity seeks to filter limited resources to fewer and fewer people in support of power and wealth. Faith communities grounded in abundance seek to make sure that everyone has enough, not just for survival but also for thriving.

Whether due to lack of information or understanding, or possibly due to willful ignorance, our current commitment to consumption and comfort is diminishing the capacity for our children, grandchildren, and future generations to thrive. Our reward is relative comfort while medicating ourselves against our growing anxiety that all might not be as we imagine it. The church contributes to this blindness when it constructs theologies that diminish our call as stewards of creation. The church's commitment to live in truth with young people begins in constructing theologies seeking God's life-giving vision for God's world.

SPEAKING HOPE

In the three to four year interlude between practicing youth ministry and seeking further theological education, I worked as an environmental planner for an engineering firm. It was an opportunity to put my undergraduate degree in geology and biology into practice while pursuing what I thought at the time would become my career. There are many great memories and important lessons from this time of investigating and writing environmental impact statements. In light of Wilson's invitation to partnership and dialogue, a particular day and a particular teacher stand out.

One morning while slogging through a muddy meadow, coring soil samples, and identifying plants, I began to think about the connections that form this particular work. During the lunch break, Dave, the wetlands biologist whom I was assisting, and I looked over the wetland we had surveyed that morning—thirteen acres of habitat that had not previously been delineated.[7] Redwing blackbirds flew through. A blue heron flying over the far edge settled into the creek, continuing a day of fishing that had begun at dawn, about the same time we began our work. "How can you look at all this," he asked, "and believe in God?" I replied "How can you see all this and not?"

Our conversation might have led to an argument over the quality of a life lived with or without belief in God, but on this day, that didn't happen. What occurred was a conversation that deepened the connection between the two of us—our mutual respect growing out of our shared love of the life found in this liminal ecological habitat. We knew this to be a place of incredible value. We were cooperating in delineating and mapping this area so it could continue to function as habitat for a wide diversity of plant, invertebrate and vertebrate species. In addition to hosting life, this wetland also served as water storage and filtration, groundwater recharge, buffer for the creek that fed it, and many other functions that it did well before our stepping in to define and protect the area. It would never be a park or refuge. It barely registered on a map, but this wetland functioned as an integral part of a larger watershed.

Dave and I guaranteed, to the best of our ability, that a proposed highway would avoid this area and cross the creek at another point with minimal impact. After his earlier question and

---

7. To delineate—We were seeking the boundaries of a wetland by sampling soils, identifying plants and looking for features indicating where water is held during the growing season in such a way that it fulfilled the Environmental Protection Agency's (EPA) and US Army Corps of Engineers standards for a protected wetland. The law has changed since this day, but wetland areas are vital for our water quality, the health of aquatic and terrestrial plant and animal species, groundwater recharge and a number of other significant purposes. At the time I did this work, wetlands protection was a high priority for federal and state governments.

my response, we entered into a long conversation about the most important aspects of our lives.

In the years prior to this conversation, I had been moving away from a rigidly constructed Christian understanding of how to make meaning. This rigid framework had been challenged by failure and success in several areas of my life. Major and minor moments of dis-equilibrium shook the narrow boxes in which I had understood faith and the place of human beings in the world.

Dave had a scientific background and a national reputation for his expertise in the field of wetland science. He articulated his growing sense of wonder through his research on the boundary communities of wetlands and their importance for the overall ecological health of aquatic and terrestrial systems. I celebrated my own work as a practical ecologist who was reminded daily of the infinite variety of life. Dave spoke of the adaptability of life in the midst of shifting water, soil, and plant economies. I tried to speak of my desire to participate in a several thousand-year-old conversation about the possibility of divine inter-relatedness with this life.

We hit a number of impasses in our conversation, but my persistent memory is our mutual respect for each other in the midst of our attempts to communicate. We spoke of our respect and love for the wonder of life and our place within it using often incommensurate vocabularies and meaning systems. However, this was not a faith versus science conversation in which each of us tried to find the epistemological trump card to prove the superiority of our language for making meaning. We both engaged in a respect for inquiry and the sacredness of life by honoring multiple perspectives, methods, and languages for making meaning. In the words of Dr. James Fowler, we both participated in practices of "faithing."[8]

This conversation opened up for me, and maybe both of us, possibilities of understanding the world and our place in it. We offered each other space for challenge and for disagreement. Though the conversation began with each of us offering the other a forced choice, it was a choice that we immediately knew was false. Dave didn't force me to choose between faith and science, he allowed me

8. Fowler, *Life Maps*, 25.

to struggle. This conversation was not limited by what we believed; it was guided by our desire to understand each other and honor the sacred mystery in our midst. Our mutual respect allowed us to engage without seeking to dismantle the argument of the other. We'd spent enough time together to know that we were not two people limited by ideology while sharing deep commitments to understanding how to participate in the creation/web of life without needing to control or consume it.

To be honest, I used to think of myself as participating in a discussion between equals; he knew the science stuff better than I did and I knew the religion stuff better than he did. However, I now suspect this wasn't true. Dave and I grew up in very similar churches, schools, and cities. Our backgrounds allowed for a closely shared religious language. He, however, had reached a point in his life when he had to leave religion in order to maintain his integrity. I had not faced the same decision, or if I had, I'd blithely skated by it.

Dave chose to treat me as an equal. Whether it was out of a sense of hospitality, his gifts as a teacher, or just his best plan for getting through the day, he opened a space of hospitality and dialogue. There's no doubt he knew significantly more about the science we practiced that day. We could easily have been done in a third of the time if he had chosen to make me his assistant rather than teach me the nuances of finding the margin between upland and wetland soils.[9]

We took core samples of the soil and determined whether the soil was aerobic or anaerobic (had bacteria that used oxygen or bacteria that could function in an oxygen depleted environment such as underwater during the growing season). We spent the morning coring, looking at a soil chart, and placing tiny wire survey flags until we had delineated about a thirteen-acre wetland from the woods and field surrounding it. It sounds tedious, and many days it was, but on that day it was a revelation. I learned more about the soil, the plants that thrived in different wetland zones, and the significance of the timing of water flow than I had learned in my previous

9. The margins of a wetland are discovered in the area where anaerobic soils meet aerobic soils, as well as a shift from wetland plants to plants adapted to drier soils. We took soil cores comparing them to standards to determine the border of the wetland. Plants were the first clue, then soil cores helped to narrow it down.

three years of practice. On that day, I was a scientist. The knowledge I brought was valued and offered a foundation for learning even more. After we'd set the soil boundaries, we had a basic idea about the flow of water through this space. Then we began to identify the plants, both within and outside the edges of the wetland. Again, while I knew several hundred plants, he took the time to teach me more, to be diligent, to see the interactions of different plants, insects, animals, and not merely speed through a checklist.

It was this careful, creative attention to the task in front of us that set the stage for our faith/science conversation. It took me several years to distinguish between faith as a possession and faith as a practice. Dave was again way ahead of me. I was in my late twenties, shaken by events in my life, holding desperately to some beliefs that defined me and therefore had to be true. Dave had grown up in an understanding of faith very close to the one I was grasping firmly and desperately defending. He told about a moment in his college career when he faced a choice, the beliefs of his faith community or the possibilities that his talent and intellectual curiosity were opening up for him at university. He found that he was an excellent young scientist and that science offered a concrete description of the world that was compelling and beautiful. He also knew the cost of this discovery. I don't know exactly how he phrased it, but it was clear in our conversation that there were folks back home who told him it was either what he was learning in school or his beliefs; both could not be "true." It was, for him, an easy choice. This choice has become for me a place of ongoing practice.

Dave's initial question was an invitation to engage life with the same integrity with which Dave approached his life. Dave's lifetime of curiosity and research into the interaction of geology, biology, physics, and chemistry within the liminal systems called wetlands grounded his open agnosticism. He asked, "How do you see all this intricate interaction of systems, living and non-living, as coming from God?" It is a question that challenged.

I grew up in a rigid understanding of Christianity that works as long as it is able to remain in an insular, monolithic community. It was a fundamentalism seeking to escape responsibility for social, political, and ecological relationships through proscription and censure. As with many forms of fundamentalism, it begins to come apart when the community's particular interpretation is confronted by diversity and difference.

I was taught that particular ways of believing, if adhered to without failing, would result in the ability to go to heaven after death. However, I first discovered wonder, mystery, and diversity through childhood explorations of the natural world. In the fervent prayers of my faithful adolescence, I remember asking God why he [sic] would create such an incredible place for us to live if the final plan was for us to all leave and join some heavenly choir filled with rigid, angry people. I preferred hiking, biking, canoeing, and fishing. I did not desire to be rescued into a place in which these activities had to be put aside in order to stand next to people I did not particularly care for and sing songs telling God something he [sic] should already know—namely how great he [sic] is for creating us and the world we had just left. It did not make a lot of sense even in my "childish" theological reasoning.

I checked Ernest Thompson Seton's *Two Little Savages*[10] out of the library over two dozen times between the ages of nine and thirteen. I read it closely every time, trying to pick up a little more woodcraft in order to see the world around me with greater depth and clarity. Seton introduced me to primary activities of my childhood, skills of listening and being still. I didn't practice them everywhere. The skills were reserved for the woods and fields that surrounded our house. I remember standing quietly in the midst of one-hundred-year-old oaks, hickories, and tulip poplars, waiting, trying to allow the life of the woods to begin again after the disturbance I had made upon entry. After a few minutes, birdsongs restarted, and then bullfrogs in our pond would tentatively thrum. Eventually, if this were a day of patience, squirrels, rabbits, snakes, and other creatures would resume their normal activities. I would then fight myself to remain still in order to see, hear, smell, and feel as much as I possibly could.

Seton's romantic characterization of Native American life was a spark to my imagination. He opened up the world for me in ways that countered the strong dispensational evangelicalism that

10. Seton, *Savages*, 1962.

formed my other primary belief system. My games exploring the world around me introduced diversity and difference into a belief system that required uniformity and rigidity. The lives and habits of the creatures living in the woods surrounding our house became the first critics of religion challenging the rigidity of my received worldview. I didn't recognize it at the time, but the practices introduced through my love of the natural world became the basis for questioning the underpinnings of a fearful faith.

In the years since, I continue to practice silence, awareness, self-reflection, and openness to the communities of life found in a variety of contexts. I began the practices anew when I worked as an environmental investigator walking corridors for proposed road and highway projects in Southern Indiana. In seminary, I discovered that these practices were woven through the Christian tradition. Through the Youth Theological Initiative (YTI) and later in the Leadership Now program at Lancaster Theological Seminary, I sought ways with other committed adults and youth to find space for practices to ground youth in faith and also offer space for embracing and critiquing the church.

Years later on a beach in South Georgia, with a group of young people, we ended our time answering big questions about our relationships in this world with a prayer. We stood together and spoke into the darkness,

> Lord it is night,
> The night is for stillness.
> > Let us be still in the presence of God.
>
> It is night after a long day.
> > What has been done has been done;
> > what has not been done has not been done;
> > let it be.
>
> The night is dark.
> > Let our fears of the darkness and of our own lives
> > rest in you.
>
> The night is quiet.
> > Let the quietness of your peace enfold us,
> > all dear to us
> > and all who have no peace.

The night heralds the dawn.
   Let us look expectantly to a new day,
   new joys,
   new possibilities.

In your name we pray.
Amen.[11]

Sustaining Practices

For the Reader—

Take a look at your personal calendar from the past year. Find the spaces where you spent time reading, thinking, or engaging questions about ecology, climate change or any other scientific field.

For your Youth—

Take a walk through your community with a group of young people. Discover what plants and animals the group can identify. Have a conversation about climate change and ecology. Ask your group where they see hope, where do they pray for hope to be revealed?

For your Faith Community—

Ask a local biologist, ecologist, or environmental scientist to your community and begin a dialogue. Start the discussion by asking how they entered into their ecological vocation. Then ask where they find hope as they think about the future.

11. New Zealand Book of Prayer, 184.

4

An Older Story

> In the beginning was God.
> And over a deep, dark, watery abyss—
> A formless void of nothingness—
> God's creative spirit swept,
> Hovering like an eagle, over her brood.
> Like a rushing wind God's spirit moved
> When it was time to create the heavens and the earth.
> And in the midst of this chaotic darkness, God spoke,
> And light, like the pulse of a quasar, came to be.[1]

THE FIRST AND LAST words of the Bible concern God's creation and celebration of our shared earth. The Bible opens with God forming the world from "nothingness" and creating the context for life. God then brings life into that space, humanity comes into existence in the world created by God for life to thrive. This is our first encounter with sacred mystery, as the stewards of God's newly spoken creation. "In the beginning," initiates a poem about the context and relationships for human thriving in the light of God's creation. The book of Revelation concludes with a vision of the new heaven and the new earth—heaven as the place where God

---

1. Reformed theologian Stephen Bouma-Prediger's poetic interpretation of the first sentences of Genesis. Bouma-Prediger, *Beauty of the Earth*, 91.

dwells and earth as the context for the thriving of all creaturely life, including human life.

The two stories of Creation that open the Christian scriptures offer themes and possibilities missed through interpretations emphasizing human dominance and exploitation Rather than setting out an understanding that human beings are created to exploit every inch of creation, these poetic narratives set the context for the still unfolding story of God's interaction with God's world.

In the first creation story,[2] God calls forth light, separating light and dark creating the cycles of growth, harvest and renewal.[3] God calls forth water and land,[4] naming Sky, Earth, and Sea,[5] holding and sustaining life spoken into existence as plants,[6] birds, fish, and animals,[7] and finally, human beings.[8]

Dr. Gene Tucker[9] writes

> The most fundamental and dominant view of the world in the Hebrew Bible is that it is God's good creation. History is the sphere in which God and human beings live out their relationship with one another in ever new, always distinct events. But those events occur in place as well as time. That place is the earth; all who live in it—plants, animals, and human beings—are creatures of God, who sustains them. Thus the Hebrew Scriptures teach its readers, as it taught Israel, to love life, and that there could be no greater blessing than to live out one's life supported by the bounty of God's gifts, especially those of creation.[10]

2. Gen 1:1—2:4.

3. Gen 1:3–4.

4. Gen 1:6.

5. Gen 1:8–10.

6. Gen 1:11–13.

7. Gen 1:20–25.

8. Gen 1:26–28.

9. Emeritus professor of Hebrew Bible, Candler School of Theology.

10. Tucker, "Peaceable Kingdom," 215.

God's delight in God's work and God's creatures is evident in the care with which God has set the context. God's declaration of humanity's being "very good" is not diminished by God's declaration of good at every step of creation. God's delight in creation is established through creating a context—an environment—for the thriving of creatures and creation in relationship.

In the Genesis narratives, humanity is called to participate in and cultivate a place of abundance, a context for all to thrive as each lives into the vocation of God's vision. Stephen Bouma-Prediger says of the first creation poem,

> In sum, this founding story affirms that God is a gracious homemaker and the earth is our home. In the first three days, the formless takes form. Because of God's creative word, from an empty void comes a habitable earth. God speaks and separates, and it comes to be. God calls and creation responds. And it is good. No cosmic battles. No primordial violence. No evil woven into the warp and weft of creation. God creates livable places for the plethora of creatures to come. And in the second three days, what is empty is filled. Again because of God's creating-sustaining word, the regions separated out from the chaotic waters are occupied by an increasingly large array of creatures: sun and moon, fish and birds, land animals both domestic and wild, and humans. God is a homemaker, showing hospitality to an increasingly diverse range of creaturely inhabitants. What was formless is given shape; what was empty is filled. Where are we? We reside with a great many other creatures on our home planet, the earth.[11]

Genesis 2:4b–25 offers a second account of creation with a different emphasis. It is a story of the creation of human beings as a distinctive moment.

> when no plant of the field was yet in the earth and no herb of the field had yet sprung up—for the Lord God had not caused it to rain upon the earth, and there was no adam to serve/work the adamah, but a flow would

11. Bouma-Prediger, *Beauty of the Earth*, 96.

well up upon the ground and water all the face of the adamah. And YHWH [by some understood as the "Breath of the World", from the sound of the letters "pronounced" with no vowels, producing only the outbreath] shaped the adam out of dust from the adamah, and blew into its nostrils the breath of life, and the adam became a living being, a breathing being.[12]

From the dust of this world we are created, and into this dust and water welling up from the earth, God breathes life. This second Creation story emphasizes the relationship between God, human beings and the stuff of this world. God breathes us into being from the dust and water of the earth. After seeing no adam (human) to work the adamah (soil), God calls human beings into existence and then places them in vocation as those who care for and work the land and share responsibility for our fellow creatures. This relationship is initiated by God's invitation for us to see and name all that God has created. To dominate or not to dominate as the focus of the interpretation of these texts misses the entire point. Adam is the designation in the text for the human being, adam is formed and respirated into life by God from adamah. The human is formed from the earth and breathed into life by YHWH, the breath of God brings to life the steward of God's Creation.[13] We aren't created to dominate and exploit, but rather to name and care for all that God has named as good. Our refusal to live into vocation and our insistence on domination and exploitation is sin.

Thomas Merton explores this idea of who we are called to be from the moment of our creation. He speaks of a moment in prayer when we know ourselves to be fully accepted and deeply connected to the rest of Creation: "In prayer we journey forward to our origin. We close our eyes in prayer and open them in the pristine moment of creation. We open our eyes to find God, his hands still smeared with clay, hovering over us, breathing into us his own divine life, smiling to see in us a reflection of himself. We go to our place of prayer confident that in prayer we transcend both place and time."[14]

12. Lamm, "Ecology in Jewish Law," vii–viii.

13. Gen 2:5–7.

14. Finley, *Merton's Palace of Nowhere*, 27.

It is in this moment of delight, of God's contemplating the beauty of God's creation that is the initiation of God's relationship with human beings. Stay for a few moments with the image of God at the moment of creation, breathing the breath of life into God's good creation. Laughing, covered in mud to the elbows, desperately in love, mother with a newborn child. Merton calls us to remember and rest as we see ourselves fully known and fully loved. This is the moment I propose we place at the forefront of an ecologically aware youth ministry.

These are not the only biblical references to God as creator and sustainer of God's good earth. God's creative engagement with the creation as the context for human beings returns to the text early in Genesis. The story turns from the goodness of God and God's creation to the refusal of human beings to live in gratitude. Adam and Eve eat a forbidden fruit, a metaphor unpacked to death. Cain slays Abel as jealous retribution arising from God's refusal of Cain's offering at the altar.

More generations arise, leading to Genesis 6, where God looks upon the earth and sees human beings descending into wickedness. A new story is told, that of Noah and a great flood. God seeks to purge human wickedness from God's earth. God has already thrown people out of the garden, condemning them to raise their food from their toil rather than partaking of the garden's abundance. Just a few generations later, the writer shows God regretting the creation of human beings. Noah and his family stand alone in the text as those worthy of remaining alive. "And God said to Noah, I have determined to make an end of all flesh, for the earth is filled with violence because of them; now I am going to destroy them along with the earth"[15] God sends Noah off to gather some lumber, build an ark, and save a few of every kind of creature. Cut to flood, waves, ark rolling in the waves, a few birds sent, and dry land rediscovered.

After Noah discerns that the earth is dry and offers sacrifices to God, God renews the covenant with human beings and fellow creatures. This re-establishment of the covenant between God and human beings leaves out the part about holding dominion and

15. Gen 6:13.

subduing the earth. That seems important, doesn't it?—the omission of this often preached dictum.

However, it is not merely the delight of God in creation that we should hold as a model for theological anthropology—our attempt to understand God's vision for full human thriving. Joseph Sittler, a twentieth-century Lutheran theologian, constructs a theological response to God's delight out of engagement with the Westminster Confession and the work of Thomas Aquinas.[16] Sittler, in his sermon "The Care of the Earth," reminds his hearers that the chief end of being human is to glorify God and *enjoy* God forever. Placing this in conversation with Aquinas' dictum that "It is of the heart of sin that humans use what they ought to enjoy, and enjoy what they ought to use,"[17] Sittler offers a frame for human beings to joyfully embrace the gifts of existence God has given by speaking into being our world and all who dwell in it.

Our joining with God through celebration of God's Creation isn't a solo pursuit. We know ourselves and find our vocation through our participation in community. Douglas John Hall's theological project is the construction of a post-Christendom understanding of the vocation of the church as contextual, ecological, and prophetic. The church's vocation begins as it speaks and lives hope as witness to the healing power of the Spirit of God in the world. Hall calls for churches to live humbly in Creation. We are creatures, as are the species that we have historically and contemporarily exploited for our own ends.

Engaging young people in the discovery of their vocation through practices of community rooted in the vocation of the church is the core of youth ministry. The ecological challenges facing this generation and generations that will follow call for a renewed vision by cultivating an ecological hermeneutic (lens) reconceiving our work in concert with God's desire for mending our world.

Youth ministry grounded in an ecological hermeneutic begins with three insights. First, we are creatures created into a context.

16. Sittler, *The Care of the Earth*, 49-62. In this sermon, Sittler challenges the abuse of the environment as evidence of deep sin and constructs the proper response as joyful engagement as creatures in God's grace-filled Creation.

17. Ibid., 49.

Created in Delight

The Genesis narratives tell of our existence created out of the earth, graced with the breath of God into life. Our story begins in communion; humans and all the other animals are created out of the same earth. Hall states that the primary cause of our world's "malaise is that the world, God's creation, is so consistently and tragically refused by the creature who is its articulate center—the human being. The creature rejects and resists its own creaturehood, and attempts to bring about alternative creations of its own."[18] Genesis emphasizes that the continuity of communion between human and God is modeled on the communion of human and all creation, and this relationship is renewed when human beings embrace their creatureliness. Hall reminds us that the divine intention initiated through God's creative act and later revealed through the person and event of Christ centers on the mending of the world.

Second, a human relationship in solidarity and mutuality with all of creation is a primary way of living the concrete Gospel of Christ. Creaturely mutuality calls human beings to form communities that resist the consumptive habits of the dominant society and celebrate our earthly context. Rituals of consumption which provide meaning in our culture are rituals reinforcing the destruction of creation and fellow creatures.

Third, a youth ministry grounded in an ecological hermeneutic should hold clearly in mind that the Gospel is grounded in God's desire for just relationships. The vocation of the church is to reclaim its prophetic voice of resistance in culture while learning to live deeply in this world. "The posture of resistance must be held in tension" with the responsibility of discipleship in the midst of a "complex worldly stewardship."[19] Hall proclaims the form of that stewardship:

> Christians who participate in the universal agape of God in Christ will know today that "the world" for which they have responsibility includes the nonhuman creatures and natural processes that are threatened by human folly and greed. They will therefore be impelled by di-

18. Hall, *Confessing the Faith*, 153.
19. Ibid., 336–7.

42

vine love to cooperate with all who share this concern for "otherkind." They will enter into covenants knowing, however, that as Christ's disciples they are not permitted to embrace outlooks and actions that reputedly "save" some species and natural processes by jeopardizing the future of others, including humanity. In other words, the holistic or integrated concern for life to which faith in Jesus Christ leads precludes the kind of specialized moral concentration that leads to myopic and exclusivist positions that in their preoccupation with parts no longer ask about the whole.[20]

Worldly stewardship calls the church into theological reflection intimately familiar with the biblical accounts, faith traditions, and the best learning of our time. The Gospel is "a disciplined reflection upon that which addresses our life and is busy changing it."[21] It is living the life of the cross through compassion for self and others. It is bearing witness into the world without the need for domination. It is standing in resistance to the powers of greed and consumption that permeate our social, political, and economic lives. It is taking responsibility for the "now" in history and participating in mending the world spoken out of the love of God.

Sallie McFague is another theologian who understands we are integrally entwined with this earth. She notes that as evident in its derivation from the Greek root *oikos*, ecology has to do with the study of our home.[22] The famous picture of the earth from space is a reminder that we live in a finite and closed system with an external energy source that provides the conditions for life to thrive. She begins theological reflection with the recognition of these limits. Her theology of embodiment takes seriously the notion of space.[23] For McFague, space includes the infinite variety of habitats that hold life in networks of biotic, chemical, and geologic relationships, the limited arena for living out relationships of health and justice, and the explicit grounded place for our existence. Her theological

---

20. Ibid., 338.
21. Ibid., 521.
22. McFague, *The Body of God*, 56.
23. Ibid., 99.

anthropology doesn't conclude with the reading of sacred texts or in the construction of philosophical categories, but continues through exploration of scientific understandings of human beings in relationship to their world. The framing story stretching our understanding of our vocation is the story of the universe.[24]

McFague echoes Karl Rahner's convictions[25] that our radical dependence on God be rewritten through an ecological vision:

> We are profoundly interrelated and interdependent with everything living and non living in the universe and especially on our planet, and our peculiar position here is that we are radically dependent on all that is, so to speak, "beneath" us (the plants on land and the microorganisms in the ocean as well as the air, water, and soil). At the same time we have become, like it or not, the guardians and caretakers of our tiny planet. In a universe characterized by complex individuality beyond our comprehension, our peculiar form of individuality and interdependence has developed into a special role for us. We are the responsible ones, responsible for all the rest upon which we are so profoundly dependent.[26]

In McFague's theological anthropology, our particular created "grandeur" is to be "self-conscious, responsible creatures" in relation to the earth and the unfolding story of God's life in relationship to the universe. Avoiding that responsibility, whether through uncontrolled greed, denying our dependence, or living blindly

24. After exploring resources for theological anthropology in the Bible and in Christian theological tradition, McFague engages the constructive narrative of the history of the ecological and theological context through Brian Swimme and Thomas Berry, *The Universe Story: From the Primordial Flaring Forth to the Ecozoic Era: A Celebration of the Unfolding of the Cosmos* (San Francisco: HarperSanFrancisco, 1992).

25. Karl Rahner, *Foundations of Christian Faith*, 128. Karl Rahner, Jesuit theologian, speaks of God's activity throughout history as a liturgy, and the revelation of God as "God's self-disclosure in a freely given intercommunion with God's people that begins at creation." The human activity of making meaning allows the human to fully become who they were created to be as he or she discovers the liturgy of God's chosen revelation through creation.

26. McFague, *The Body of God*, 109.

without any awareness of our responsibility at all, is sin.[27] McFague's eco-theological anthropology requires that we also begin to refer to ourselves as co-creatures, transforming our understanding as co-creators, in dependent responsibility with, and in service to our fellow creatures and the world upon which we all depend for our shared life.

All of this isn't an attempt to reinvent Christianity, but a desire to disentangle it. Sittler, Hall, McFague, Bouma-Prediger, and many other theologians with an ecological hermeneutic are challenging the church and the practices of faith to leave the privileges of empire and engage the early mission of the church, the renewal of the world.

N. T. Wright, New Testament scholar and Bishop of Durham, affirms that the movement in the Christian church toward an ecological hermeneutic is a return to the mission of the church, rather than the invention of a new green mission. However, many contemporary interpretations tend to proclaim the end of faith as going home to heaven, and the earth is seen as a place to be left behind.

So powerful is this belief in a great deal of popular preaching, liturgy, and hymns that it comes as a shock to many people to be told that this is simply not how the earliest Christians saw things. For early Christians, the resurrection of Jesus launched God's new creation upon the world, beginning the fulfillment of the prayer that Jesus taught his followers in which God's kingdom would come 'on earth as in heaven' and anticipating the 'new heavens and new earth' promised by Isaiah and promised again in the New Testament.[28]

Rita Nakashima Brock and Rebecca Anne Parker open up this vision of mission in *Saving Paradise: How Christianity Traded a Love of this World for Crucifixion and Empire*. They dive deep into the history of Christianity and find a consistent desire to live into God's paradise, not as a place of perfection or utopian vision, but as communities seeking the persistent presence of God's love for the world. Brock and Parker find a theology different from "longing for a pristine past and judging the present to be a corrupt age."[29] They follow the thread of historic faith that falls in love with God's world

27. Ibid., 113.

28. Wright, "Jesus is Coming," I-72.

29. Brock and Parker, *Saving Paradise*, 416.

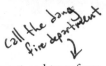

because we can't "lament and transform . . . what we reject or deny or refuse to engage."[30] Brock and Parker conclude with a call that should resonate with anyone committed to the lives of young people and a desire for life in the vision of God's abundant goodness.

> Sustaining communities must be at the forefront of our work, and we must accept that we have power and responsibility to foster life in them. To be both powerful and responsible requires us to be committed to the sometimes difficult, sometimes joyful relationship of human communities. They are the only way we come to perceive and act upon the world for greater good that both includes and transcends our individual existence . . .
>
> Communities of ethical grace sustain relationships that require us to share responsibility, act generously toward one another, and resist oppressive dominating forces that separate human beings from each other and deny our powers of love and friendship. They value the distinctive gifts of individuals for the good of the whole and require us to be open and vulnerable to the many complex dimensions of life that support the survival and thriving of life on earth, in all its diversity.[31]

Ministry with youth and young adults that begins in reclaiming the delight of God in creation invites young people into "communities of ethical grace": life giving spaces where they can discover their vocation in community and offer it for the life of the world.

Brock and Parker conclude with a vision and invitation that reframes how we might reconstruct Bacigalupi's banquet for generations as we partner with young people in renewing faith and building ethical community.

> We reenter this world-as-sacred-space when we love life fiercely, and in the name of love, protect the goodness of earth's intricate web of life in all its manifold forms. We feast in paradise when we open our hearts to lamentation, to amplitudes of grief for all that has been lost and cannot be repaired. The beloved departed who have

30. Ibid.

31. Ibid., 418.

come before us draw near. The veil lifts between the living and the dead. We recommit ourselves to this world as holy ground when we remember the fullness of life that is possible through our communities, our life-affirming rituals, and our love of beauty. Thus immersed, we are more responsive to and responsible for life in this world. We give thanks for gifts of love that have been ours all along, and ever-widening circle of beauty, the Spirit in life. We enter fully— heart, mind, soul and strength— into savoring and saving paradise.[32]

The goodness of creation is written into the beginning and the end of the biblical texts. It is found in the Psalms, in the prophets, in the teachings of Jesus. It is foundational to the good news that the church seeks to proclaim for the world. Genesis begins with two articulations of the creative grace of God calling all that 'is' into being. Revelation concludes the canon with a vision of a new heaven and a new earth, all the life of the new earth nourished by the river of life flowing from God's throne in heaven; a river nurturing life in the new earth God has gifted to God's creatures. As Merton reminded us, it is in the midst of this creative activity that we find God in celebration and delight for all of Creation. Learning to see through an ecological hermeneutic isn't a drift from biblical Christianity; it is a return to partnership with God in creative action for the world.

Sustaining Practices

For the Reader—

Take a morning, find a spot for rest, reflection, maybe your favorite morning beverage. Read Stephen Bouma-Prediger's paraphrase of the Genesis creation story. Sit back, seek the image of God at the moment of creation, is she laughing with joy?

32. Ibid., 420.

For your Youth—

Bring Bouma-Prediger's paraphrase of the Creation narrative to a youth Bible study and ask folks to take it home as the week's scripture for study. Return the following week for the study time. Take as many weeks as you need to work through the text and any resistance to reading a non-standard paraphrase of the Bible.

For your Faith Community—

Probably should have told their parents what you were doing at Bible study. Just kidding, better idea than doing the study with youth, bring adults and young people together to read and study Bouma-Prediger's paraphrase. If possible move from this text to Thomas Berry and Brian Swimme's *Universe Story* and/or resources from the Center for the Story of the Universe at http://www.story oftheuniverse.org.

5

Peregrinations

ONCE AGAIN I SAT down in front of the computer, read the work written the past few days and hit delete. Looking at the blank screen, I know I have things to say, but, well, the right words aren't arriving in the right order. I stand up, put on my hat (a signal to my dogs that we're heading out) and grab four leashes. After exuberant canine rituals provoked by my actions, we walk out the front door. Lexi, my border collie, walks to the corner and turns left. We head back into our neighborhood, my dogs and our four or five walks a day have deepened my knowledge of this place and my neighbors. The pack senses that smells have shifted since walking this same route earlier in the day and suspects that the squirrels have become a bit too comfortable.

I walk and think this book through one more time. There is no debate in the scientific community that human activity has changed the baseline for our world's climate. Climate change is merely one of many challenges emerging as human beings discover the limits of living on a finite planet with finite resources. Paulo Bacigalupi's image of dinner enjoyed by one generation while the next pays the bills is a metaphor for our time. The biblical narrative calls its followers to live in careful relationship with our created context and fellow creatures. All of this seems to work as a compelling case for changing our behavior, but then I think of the half-dozen scientific reports I'd read in the past week detailing how in spite of all this, we are increasing our consumption of everything, increasing pressure on the systems sustaining life. I turn a corner, wondering how I'll bridge any of these swirling thoughts back to hope.

I walk by my neighbors' houses. Our town's history is illustrated as I walk from block to block. I live in a house built in 1911, as I move closer to the center of the city I move from American foursquare houses of the 1910s past a few Victorians to the older brick facades of the late 1800s. Our downtown has a number of buildings from the 1880s and earlier. I keep walking, past old churches, an ice cream shop, a bookstore, down to the coffee shop. If I walked further south I'd enter a liberal arts college—founded in 1842—or to the west, the high school and middle school. The houses, downtown, and college campus all conform to images of an idyllic Midwestern town.

On March 20, 2012, I left the house to walk in 83-degree heat—a reminder of the ecological shifts described earlier in this work. It was the first day of spring, and all over the USA, high temperature records were being shattered, some places were as much as 20 degrees above any previous record. We are living into Bill McKibben's *Eaarth*, his designation for our world as it shifts to the new reality. The year 2010 was tied with 2005 as the hottest year on record,[1] 2012 is starting out as if it will set the new record.[2] Simple solutions such as recycling, driving a hybrid, or turning down the thermostat might offer a brief moment of personal satisfaction but don't shift the arc of our locust culture, a culture that perceives the world as food for its insatiable appetite. These easy practices support our lifestyle rather than calling it into question. We have to cultivate thinking and practices that allow us to more deeply live into the world as it is, reconstructing communities for the life of the world, inviting young people into living into vocation. Youth and young

1. NOAA, "2010 Tied for Warmest Year."

2. The twelve-month period from July 2011 to June 2012 is now listed on the NOAA website, http://www.noaa.gov/, as the hottest ever. This assessment will be studied and refined over the next year, possibly to be superseded if projections hold true for 2012–13 weather patterns predicted by NOAA and other world government climate agencies.

adult ministry grounded in ecological practices cultivates thinking beyond acquisition, consumption, domination, and destruction.

Ecological practices are essential for participating responsibly in ministry with youth and young adults. I've tried to outline the dire path our exploitation of resources and perverse sense of entitlement are carving for generations to come. We are living into the world Andrew Revkin, James Hansen, Bill McKibben, and many others have warned of and described. My generation is the last to sit at the head of Bacigalupi's banquet, generations following will pay the bill. This still doesn't answer the question—what do we do? Christianity is lived into the life of the world, a healthy faith is action and contemplation in vital relationship, with a commitment to seeing clearly oppression and injustice while working diligently to change the world. What can be done when it seems as if nothing can be done? We have to begin to imagine and invite young people into "little moves against destructiveness."[3]

Wangari Maathi, founder of the Green Belt movement in Africa and recipient of the 2004 Nobel Peace Prize offers a parable from the Quechuan people illustrating the urgency of our environmental crisis. The forest has been set on fire and all of the animals flee the advancing flames. The hummingbird, in despair that her home and the home of all the animals is being destroyed, tries to rally a response to fight the fire. She is rebuffed. The animals sit at a safe distance, watching the fire, despairing that all is lost. The hummingbird flies to a nearby stream and takes a drop of water in her beak. She flies to the fire and spits the drop of water on an ember. The other animals call out to her, "you're wasting your time, why do you bother?" The hummingbird persists, time and time again, taking a drop in her beak and returning to put it on the raging fire.

Now here is where the story gets interesting. As with many folktales, it has many possible endings. Sometimes the hummingbird persists while the animals with much larger capacity for fighting the fire sit by and watch, continuing to tell the hummingbird that she is wasting her time. Other times, the example of the hummingbird

---

3. Hallie, *Lest Innocent Blood Be Shed*, 85.

inspires or shames the rest of the animals into action.[4] It is a living story asking those who hear it to write an ending through their actions. Earlier chapters sketched our world on fire, everyday we have many opportunities to decide how we will respond.

Our culture has either chosen to ignore the huge challenges we are creating for the thriving of future generations, or if not ignore, to approach these challenges with unthinking optimism. This optimism supports the idea that we can increase our consumption of resources in a finite world and that simplistic solutions—recycling, hybrid cars, insulating McMansions, etc.—will change the outcome.

Another simplistic support for inaction is found in the dispensational eschatology underlying a significant portion of North American theology. At its worst this theology is found in the *Left Behind* books, offering 'believers' a way to avoid environmental responsibility by seeing the destruction of God's good creation as an element in God's plan. Adherents of this particular worldview have to ignore the context of the texts they quote to frame their position that the chosen will be taken to heaven while the cursed (everyone who doesn't agree with their politics, theology, and nihilistic worldview) are 'left behind.' While this is the most perverse articulation of a heretical Christian nihilism, there are degrees of escapist eschatology underlying a wide swath of theologies that make peace with consumerism at the expense of stewardship.

Barbara Rossing, professor of New Testament at the Lutheran School of Theology at Chicago, takes apart this contemporary heresy in *The Rapture Exposed*. She engages the primary texts that dispensational hucksters claim as proof of their position and finds a very different narrative, one that supports God's continuing care for God's creation. She finds, particularly in the prophetic texts in Revelation, the invitation to "explore ways we can understand our reign not as domination but as sharing in God's healing of the world."[5] Rossing's conclusion echoes Sallie McFague's core theological theme that our existence is intimately tied to this world.

4. Yahgulanaas, *Flight of the Hummingbird.*
5. Rossing, *Rapture Exposed*, 158.

As discussed in the previous chapter, Sallie McFague reminds us that when we study ecology, we study our home. The earth is vulnerable, vital, alive and the place created for life to thrive. This vulnerability and vitality is emphasized through McFague's metaphor of the earth as God's body. McFague draws from multiple theological and ecological sources in her construction of the metaphors of the earth as our home and also the body of God.

Barry Commoner, in his book *The Closing Circle*, outlines four basic laws for understanding ecology:

1. Everything is Connected to Everything Else

2. Everything Must Go Somewhere

3. Nature Knows Best

4. There Is No Such Thing as a Free Lunch[6]

Everything is connected—my life, my neighbors' lives; my house, my neighbors' houses; my dogs and all the creatures of our shared habitat. The connections are positive and negative, visible and invisible. Our awareness of our reliance on each other and the world we inhabit is the foundation of an ecological hermeneutic. We seek to become more aware of how we impact each other through our waste and our decisions to limit that waste. An ecological hermeneutic is rooted in understanding the abundance of the natural world and seeking to cultivate that abundance.

We cultivate an ecological hermeneutic by relearning, or possibly learning for the first time, a vocabulary for the world we inhabit. We re-read, or read for the first time, the texts and practices that we've conformed to our consumer culture now seen through an ecological lens. We re-form, or form for the first time, communities committed to living for the health of our world. Ecologically aware ministries are engaged with generations who have gone before while remaining mindful of generations who will follow. Faith formation in an ecologically mindful youth and young adult ministry discerns the life-giving narratives arising from the faithful generations of our past while discerning new ways to live into the abundance of God's world in faith with generations to come.

6. Commoner, *The Closing Circle*, 29–42.

My earlier walk was one of hundreds over the past few years, leaving my front door with my dogs to try to work through the last thing I read or next thing to write. This work is an invitation to think differently about young people, faith communities and our shared responsibility for the world. An ecological hermeneutic challenges us to renew our understanding concerning our place in the world. The houses I walk by, my neighbors' homes, are connected to the land upon which they sit. The actions of my neighbors affect our shared community, both human and more-than-human. The waste we all produce impacts how we live together, even as that waste is placed on the curb and carted out of sight.

The task of my generation, the generations who follow and generations yet to be born is to live into our vocation as stewards and our relationships as fellow creatures as we rediscover the promise of God's abundance. If the church embraces this task, then it will become the church that can carry faith forward for generations yet to come. If the church chooses to ignore the great work of this vocation—or tries to maintain a neutral position while the seas rise, creatures die, and crops fail—then for the health of the world and the thriving of generations, young people will need to leave the church.

As I tried to say earlier, churches seeking to attract and keep young people are asking the wrong questions in pursuit of the wrong answers. If the church is to become a community of faithful change in our new ecological reality it needs to renew its mission as people who seek to live faithfully into hope beyond escape and unthinking optimism in the midst of economic and ecological exile. Walter Brueggemann reminds us that "exile, a context of despair becomes the venue in which these incredible new commitments of God are made and the world is under God's promises."[7] He believes that "the prophetic promises function in scripture to keep us imagining futures that God intends to bring among us . . . our work in faith is to be open to the impetus of these new possibilities."[8]

7. Brueggemann, "Hope and Imagination." This is a film interview with Walter Brueggemann found as a resource on the liturgical resources website Work of the People.

8. Ibid.

The Holy Spirit is "God's force of newness which is so important in a technological society that wants to stop all of that and control everything."[9] Faith should be a practice that opens us always anew to the fresh movement of God in the world. It is a way into imagination, holding out hope for God's renewal and abundance. This has to be a lived reality for the foundation of a church that is worthy of young people. A church arising out of the historical witness, seeking to be faithful for the life of generations yet to be born.

Our species is building a world that threatens our very survival. We are pushing life-sustaining systems past the equilibrium that allowed our species and our fellow creatures to evolve and thrive. In April of 2012, scientists measured CO_2 levels at 400 ppm in the Arctic:[10] this is a level not found in the 800,000 year record preserved in the ice. As I've said several times in this work, and as is said dozens of times every week by the scientific community, the window for shifting the arc of consumption and ecological devastation is rapidly closing. There doesn't appear to be the social pressure or political will necessary for shrinking our consumption down to sustainable levels. Our planet is becoming a place of exile for generations to come. It is imperative that people of faith begin to build resilient communities seeking ways for all creatures to thrive.

Sustaining practices

For the Reader—

Walk around your neighborhood, take notes on who you know and what you know about the products and energy that enters and the waste that leaves. Think about the connections you and your neighbors have to each other and fellow creatures.

9. Ibid.
10. NOAA, "Carbon dioxide levels reach milestone at Arctic sites."

Created in Delight

For your Youth—

Host a similar hike around your parish with your youth in the area around the church or a nearby neighborhood.

For your Faith Community—

Bring what you've found to your faith community and begin to think how you might be better neighbors to all.

6

Living into Seeing

CLOSE THIS BOOK AND go outside. Or, if you happen to be reading outside (good!) then close the book and look around you. What do you see? Plants, animals, birds, bugs, worms, toads, turtles, etc.? How much of what you see can you name with its common name or name by genus and species? What do you see and what do you know well enough to name?

I'm sitting outside under a one-hundred-year-old maple, it's a cool morning in June, about 70 degrees Fahrenheit at ten o'clock. Birds are chattering above me. I recognize chickadees and the dreaded English House Sparrow, maybe a Robin, but I'm not sure. I've got three raised beds in my backyard, all need weeding, but the lettuce is coming on and the chard, planted late, is starting to look like it might supplement a few meals. I've got a short row of fingerling potatoes flowering behind the chicken wire that protects the raised beds. Chicken wire is required since my dogs believe themselves to be much better gardeners than the evidence supports.

Maeve, one of my Aussies lies under a blue homemade picnic table that was ready for the dump when I moved here four years ago. I know the arguments for tossing or composting it, but it remains because the dogs have turned the ground beneath into a favorite cool spot. My backyard, like my small side and front yards, are neighborhood embarrassments. Many of my neighbors grow native plants instead of grass in their front yards, but I don't organize the purple coneflower, New England aster and other plants beyond an occasional purge of noxious weeds. My side yard is a chaotic planting of gray-headed coneflower, purple catchfly, bee balm and Black-eyed Susans—my forty square foot prairie.

Even a casual observer could come to a few conclusions about my place and maybe my character. I am a careless gardener and housekeeper. I have much bigger hopes than resources, and perhaps more resources than clarity of vision. My dogs are more important than my garden and tend to herd me as their only wayward sheep. I can name some of the plants that surround me, the red maple overhead, red oak out front, and a riot of asters in the front flower beds. But there are many more plants I have no name for besides "flower," "shrub" or "weed." The same is true of local animals, Lexi, Maeve, Copper, and Scout—a border collie and three Australian Shepherds laying about the backyard. I know of one or two wary squirrels living in the maple and a few midwestern birds. But there are many more creatures of which I am unaware. I am learning this place, but I know almost nothing about its many inhabitants.

Seeing, naming, and parsing the relationships of the world around us are initial steps toward a relationship of responsible stewardship. The first step is as easy as walking outside to discover the species of the nearest tree or plant. The more we see and learn the names of our fellow creatures, the better we can live in responsible relationship. Living into the vocation of stewardship is the act of growing in love for what we are meant to love. The practices of seeing, learning, and loving God's creation shift our objectifying view of the world from resources to be used to creatures and relationships to be nurtured. These are core practices of spiritual formation. These practices are small steps toward remembering our place in creation and our relationship with our fellow creatures.

I don't know how we might solve the problems that will arise as we enter into a time of changed climate and discovery of our limits. The problems are too large and our resources for addressing them are diminishing. However, this isn't a reason for despair. I will repeat what I said earlier: to be a follower of Jesus Christ is to choose to be constrained by hope rather than consumed by despair. We can turn to the places we live with a commitment to action and

[handwritten margin note: like people we cannot love what we learn to love]

a desire for healing. We begin by discovering our contexts and our fellow creatures. From this beginning we partner with others in seeking healing of our shared land.

Our environmental challenges necessitate that we seek to rebuild community, not save our institutions. I propose that we all enter into an extended time of discernment about our relationships to word and world. This time of discernment could offer a foundation for reinterpreting our place in Creation, challenging our understanding of faith and opening our subsequent desire to live into our vocation. An ecological hermeneutic grounded in this practice of discernment challenges commitments to consumerism and institutionally focused understandings of success. Whether or not denominations and associated institutions choose to engage faith through an ecological hermeneutic, the earth's systems demand that it become the foundational practices of ministry with youth and young adults.

This is a move toward practices that seek to disrupt what we believe rather than reinforce unexamined beliefs. We live in a time that allows us to understand our lives separate from our environment. This is an incredible privilege as long as we can ignore the consequences of lives lived without regard to our environment or concern for our fellow creatures. The practice of learning to recognize the other living creatures surrounding us also allow us to begin to see the stresses threatening the lives of our fellow creatures. We are building a reference base so that we can recognize a shift in the ecologies we need for our thriving and the health of our fellow creatures.

You might need to take a breather. I've tried to tell the truth as best I can discern. It's a lot to take in for the first time, or be reminded of if you are actively avoiding recognition of how bad our ecological situation is. Step outside, find a place to rest. Lean against a tree, sit on a park bench, lie next to a lake or stream. What is alive and near? Take a guide with you and begin to learn the names of the plants, animals and minerals native to your place. Once you've learned the names of species common to your local context, begin to learn those in your region. With our basic vocabulary, we can begin to (re)learn languages that describe relationships we have previously neglected or chosen to ignore. The languages of which I am speaking include not only ecology and the sciences, but also a renewed reading of the texts that shape the Christian faith. The texts call us to responsibility for the life of this world as we embrace our status as creatures in Creation.

How might we shape ministries with young people that seek the thriving of all creatures? What beliefs, practices, and structures of discipleship sustain life? What beliefs, practices, and structures diminish the capacity for life to thrive? Maathi's parable offers little hope for easy solutions, but it does offer a vision for cultivating hope in the midst of overwhelming challenge. The next moves are small ones, little moves against destructiveness.

The small step of learning to see our connections to the health of our world is an essential movement toward critically engaging beliefs, practices and structures underlying our lives. Our critical engagement seeks to cultivate creaturely imagination, relational stewardship and gratitude in our lived contexts. Then we can begin the reconstruction of our rituals and practices aware of our world and seeking God, creator, sustainer, and redeemer.

In the summers of 1998 to 2000 I led small groups of young adults in exploring connections between faith and ecology on one of the Georgia Sea Islands. Almost all the students who participated were alumni from the summer academy of the Youth Theological Institute (YTI) of the Candler School of Theology at Emory University. These retreats began with the same core assumptions about teaching and learning in community that also guided the YTI summer academy. Primarily, the idea is that a community of youth and adults benefit by gathering to explore the nature of faith and participate in faith practices together. In our safe space all questions were okay, especially questions about how God is perceived, experienced, imagined, and celebrated. We gathered as a community to participate in social practices (the practices of various human communities) and social realities (such as race, class, and gender) imagining new possibilities and opportunities for faith formation. Our teaching/learning communities sought to encounter people (biographies, living individuals, and communities) whose lives and work have been shaped by their faith convictions. Our YTI community also played with transformational practices of worship, prayer, and contemplation as experimental modes for being church as well as engaging in service, embodying care for the world as a response to our deepening faith.

One of the concluding sentences in the YTI mission statement was the desire that YTI would become a mentoring community for the sustained practice of integrating theology and social criticism. These alumni retreats arose out of a desire to re-establish relationships and offer a community for further theological and critical reflection.

In time, as we learned more about the experiences of our alumni we found that the desire for authentic relationships and meaningful conversations taken for granted at YTI were deeply desired in our faith communities. This hunger sparked some to create similar spaces within their congregations or faith communities, places that have many more resources and opportunities than a small summer youth program or retreat.

The ecology retreats were eight days focused on exploring connections between faith and ecology. The retreats took place on Sapelo Island just off the coast of Georgia. Sapelo lies in the South Atlantic Bight—the concave curve of coastline extending from Cape Hatteras, North Carolina to Miami, Florida. The tides range up to six feet and generate a dynamic system of salt marshes that serve as a breeding and nursery grounds for Atlantic fisheries. The tides also governed our time on retreat by determining when we could paddle, seine, or even travel to or from certain areas of the island.

There is something about connecting ourselves to the patterns of nature

Sapelo has a long history of human habitation. Near the western shore stands a large shell ring, evidence that rich oyster beds in the adjoining bays sustained human habitation more than three thousand years ago. The Spanish established a mission for a short time in late 1500s to early 1600s. Prior to the Civil War, the island was a cotton and timber plantation. After the Civil War, up to five communities thrived on the island, making their living from fishing, crabbing, oysters, and timber. In the late 1800s, Thomas Spalding bought the bulk of the island, planting sugar cane and selling live oak for shipbuilding. In 1911, Howard Coffin, founder of the

Hudson Motor Company, bought the island from the Spalding family. He expanded the road system, introduced cattle, and renovated and expanded the island mansion. In 1933, R. J. Reynolds purchased the land, expanded the mansion and other buildings, and moved people from several villages to Hog Hammock so that he could establish a personal hunting preserve. He introduced deer, pigs, bear, and other game animals not native to the island. In 1965, the Reynolds family donated their land to the state of Georgia.

Today, Sapelo Island is lightly inhabited with two primary human communities. Many inhabitants of the first, Hog Hammock, trace their family's residence to deeds granted by General Sherman at the conclusion of the Civil War. The second group is made up of researchers working in the ecological research station run jointly by the state department of natural resources and the University of Georgia. All of these elements were in the mix as we explored how the contexts of our formation shape our formation.

Our teaching and learning community formed before we arrived on the island. During the van ride there, we held a conversation about how we wanted to engage the elements of the course and what relationship we wanted to have with time. On Sapelo, we had choices—did we want to be driven by our watches, did we want to move when we felt like it, or did we want to find other ways to understand time? I began the conversation by asking, "How do you want to become aware of the times of the island?" "What do you mean by 'times?'" Jennie broke in, somewhat prompted by a discussion she and I had the previous week about her experience on a semester study abroad, and said, "I think we are talking about trying to locate some rhythms. Rhythm might be a better word than time, because time is caught up with clocks, watches, and schedules. I think of rhythms and I think of my body and I think of how the sun comes up every day. When I was in India, we made sure that we were able to begin the day when the sun did. We started every morning by watching the sunrise. I don't necessarily want to get up at sunrise every day but I do think we should try to begin our day when the island is waking. I think we should think about an early morning start."[1]

From this we talked about when to rise, how we wanted to begin each day, the influence of weather and tides on our plans, and other ways of understanding that time on the island would have a different character from our homes or previous teaching/learning contexts.

Our first practice after arriving on the island by our own power in kayaks[2] was to discover. Easy questions shaped our conversation—what's that tree? Southern Live Oak. What's hanging from it? Spanish Moss. Oh and those little red spider creatures are mites, yeah put that down. What's growing up the trunk of the tree? Resurrection fern, hope we get some rain, it looks amazing when it greens out. What are these red bugs crawling up my arm? They're mites living in the Spanish moss, told you to put that down!

We also asked each other questions to discern what we might already know about this particular place. Has anyone ever been to a Georgia sea island? What trees, shrubs, flowers, grasses, and vegetation do you recognize? What mammals, birds, insects, amphibians, arachnids, etc., are familiar? The initial practice on the island was to spark our curiosity by generating questions to discover what we knew and where we were ignorant about this new place. It was not important that the group knew much, the primary project of our time together was to put names to things and watch how creatures and contexts interacted. We pulled out the field guides, grounding texts for understanding the world around us.

As you begin this work with young people, go to a local bookstore and purchase some field guides for your area of the country. Put them on the bookshelf in the space where you gather with youth. Put them next to the Bibles, songbooks and other youth resources you have in that space. As young people begin to discern what they know, they are often surprised at the knowledge base on which they can build. We aren't able to discern change or cultivate

1. Conversation reconstructed from field notes.

2. This retreat was offered three summers, the first year we paddled to and from the island, the second and third years we rode the ferry over and paddled home at the end of the week.

relationship with abstractions about a hurting world; ecological knowledge begins in local knowledge.

After you get your field guides go outside, any season, and look. What's there? Concrete? trees? A dandelion growing up through a crack in the sidewalk? Now walk a few blocks or a quarter mile, describe all that you see that's alive, what you can name and what is still unknown. Write it down. This is a start to (re)learning the world around you. In time try to establish relationships with people who are familiar with the places you frequent. Begin to work with a local naturalist or ecologist as part of your ministry. Have them lead a hike in a local park as part of a youth group meeting.

On our Sapelo retreats, we spent one or two days learning with a local ecological educator. We studied with Taylor Schoettle, who had recently retired as an educator for the Sapelo Island research station of the University of Georgia. He'd written two books on the ecology of the Georgia barrier islands, one of which we used as a resource. Taylor's enthusiasm for this small place off the coast of south Georgia was contagious. I'd chosen Sapelo because it was relatively close to Atlanta and offered a dynamic, but not pristine environment. Taylor was a local naturalist and writer who ran day trips for school children during the year and was a bit apprehensive about working with a group of religiously minded young adults. His enthusiasm and the group's curiosity made for a wonderful working relationship.

Taylor taught by introducing students to animal and plant species characteristic of a particular habitat. For example, fiddler crabs and marsh grass in the salt marshes. He then built relationships through our new knowledge of these species to others that live within their ecological niche. Taylor maintained a rapid pace throughout several habitats on the island, weaving the inter-relationship of systems and species with the consequences of human impacts. Though he had studied the islands for decades, Taylor remained open to wonder and beauty found in the world around him. Witnessing his deep love for the habitats and creatures he knows intimately was as powerful a lesson as the introduction to new species and their interactions.

Each new habitat became the place of discovery, of delight. We explored a small tidal pool as the tide went out, discovering minnows,

beautiful

tiny crustaceans, shrimp, crabs, and maybe the larva or eggs of a larger ocean going species. Taylor would bend down, point to something none of us had noticed, his eyes would light up and he would begin to explain the significance of this tiny creature and its place in the ecological system we were exploring. Each discovery, illustrated by Taylor's wonder, reinforced the significance of our knowing about the creatures and the contexts in which they were found.

We began to learn this place together. Exploring the behavior of small crabs in the marsh, beginning to discern the differences in vegetation as the water moved from fresh to brackish to salt water over in small areas. We found alligator wallow holes, and saw the eyes of residents. We slowly began to see the island.

A couple of days after our time with Taylor, we paddled our kayaks from Sapelo down a meandering inter-island channel to Blackbeard Island, a National Wildlife Refuge. It is a context that complicated our understanding of the 'natural world.' It is beautiful, austere, and seemingly pristine, but the natural species and habitats are under intense pressure from non-native species such as deer and wild pigs. There are few, if any, natural predators for these species. Blackbeard's claim to fame, beyond its wildlife refuge status, is the annual fall hunts it hosts in order to keep the non-native species at somewhat manageable populations. The walk on Blackbeard offered a number of opportunities for talking about the character of human interaction with our planet.[3]

We also spent time with a local historian, touring the community, listening to stories from Gullah-Geechee culture. One afternoon was spent making baskets with local craftswomen, allowing stories of their craft and life on the island to invite us to a deeper relationship with this new place. Each activity framed another way of practicing our engagement with the human/ecological contexts of the island. The entire retreat can be summed up as observing and parsing the contexts of ecological observation and theological

---

3. I am neither for nor against hunting. I think that careful hunters have become a primary predator, keeping a number of species from destroying habitats. Since we've destroyed most predators in the habitats in which we live, we have to have other ways of maintaining the balance of prey and predator species for the thriving of all.

reflection. Slowly, we engaged practices of discerning and living in relationship in this new context. The unfamiliarity of Sapelo prompted us to expose assumptions about living in our home ecological contexts. My hope was that we would continue the practices of seeing deeply, asking questions, and changing behavior as we returned to our homes. For a couple of years after the retreats, several students continued to write and meet to work on a collection of photographs and reflections about Sapelo in dialogue with experiences in their home habitats.[4]

Our time of retreat on Sapelo opened our perceptions, practices, and narratives. Learning to pay attention to our bodies as they moved through a new place, and all the different smells, sounds, tastes and sensations on our skin, helped us reconnect to kinesthetic ways of learning. Educational philosopher Maxine Greene described the importance of immersion in the arts in a similar way. "At the very least, participatory involvement with many forms of art can enable us to see more in our experience, to hear more on normally unheard frequencies, to become conscious of what daily routines have obscured, what habit and convention have suppressed."[5] On our retreat, we sought to enter with the same openness into our learning with the world surrounding us. We were surrounded by the artistry of the Creator through the stories and crafts of the people who lived on Sapelo. We were led to deep appreciation for the beauty of all the island's creatures and communities.

There are many voices decrying the loss of connection to our world. Many times these laments are focused on young people, as if they alone have constructed ways for separating themselves from the world around them. This sense of separation is a place of frustration for young people as well as adults. Learning the names and relationships of the world in which we live is a primary action of living faithfully in relationship to the Creator and creation.

In the evening, when the light grew low on the marsh, we would gather and reflect on the lessons of the day. Where had we felt the stirrings of our own connection to this world? What were

4. These retreats concluded when funding ran out and my academic obligations took me away from Atlanta.

5. Greene, *The Dialectic of Freedom*, 123.

our bodies telling us about our day's work? What reminders came that our wholeness was found in all aspects of mind, body, spirit? This was the initiation of a reflective conversation seeking to bring the events and lessons of the day into synthesis as a learning community. The reflection conversation is a sifting and probing into shared and conflicting values. It requires honest engagement in a safe, sometimes uncomfortable conversation.

Our discussion times ended with silence. We finished the initial reflection time, talking about hopes for the week, anxieties, and commitments and then entered into a time of quiet until the conclusion of breakfast.[6] Silence is an important step in the process of learning the names of things. The practice of silence can occur in a variety of ways, it may simply be pausing when you wake to listen to the world waking around you. Or it might require setting aside time every day without any devices that connect us to the constant flow of information that characterizes many of our lives.

The intent was to end our day slowly, listening closely, using all our senses, allowing ourselves to enter into rhythm as the marsh surrounding us shifted from day to night. Rather than one last conversation, or night hike or . . . whatever the next anxious moment we might be tempted to insert to close our day, we chose to allow the possibility of slowing ourselves into the space we inhabited. The practice of silence allowed a space to open for entry into the contexts that we often take for granted. It also provided an opportunity to begin to reclaim voice. This may seem as if the opposite would be true, but silence chosen, allows for personal power not available when silence is imposed or masked by chatter. This was a goal, but some nights we found other ways to remain aware of who we were and our relationship to the world we inhabit.

Late one night, we stopped our walk on the beach and lay down in the sand. We all lost our breath at the same time.

6. This was loosely enforced. As a caution, I would say all of these suggested guidelines are only good if the community agrees to them. If they are set up as the rules they become points of resistance and will hamper rather than nurture learning. I try to set a tone encouraging these outcomes. I'd speak with a couple of students prior to the trip, ask them what their hopes were and talk about the possibility that practices of listening and seeing were at the core of our learning together.

"Oh!"

We stared up into a sky without light pollution. We saw the skies people saw before artificial lights dimmed the night.

"Let's just lay here and look up at the stars."

"Or lay here and look down into the universe." Clay went on to say "I have a friend who said gravity holds us to the skin of this planet or we'd all fall down into the stars."

We lay there for a couple of hours talking, thinking, imagining who we might be, small and vulnerable, big and powerful, in relationship to the beauty in which we perceived ourselves to be immersed. We wrestled with meaning, faith, disappointment and hope. We were exposed to the universe. I probably spoke too much that night—it tends to happen—but what I remember was a wash of holy gratitude that I was there, with these people, on that night. They shaped me. They helped to form my thought, not just in that moment, but throughout our experiment in ecological exploration. We loved the universe, this world and each other into places that brought faith into reality.

Looking down into our galaxy, the Milky Way reframed our place in the world. We're not the center of all that exists; even in our galaxy we're at its edge on a tiny planet in the midst of magnificent beauty, significant but not the center. We're capable of awe, full desire to seek the breath of God in all our existence; we are also capable of awful destruction and exploitation in the name of God. We can join with God seeking the healing of God's world or we can manifest our narcissistic domination of creation for our wealth and comfort.

That night we found ourselves suspended between the embers and the stars articulated so beautifully by Erazím Kohák.

> Quietly the darkness grows in the forest, seeping into the clearing and penetrating the soul, all-healing, all-reconciling, renewing the world for a new day. Were there no darkness to restore the soul, humans would quickly burn out their finite store of dreams. Unresting, unreconciled, they would grow brittle and break easily, like an oak flag dried through the seasons. When electric glare takes away all the reconciling night, the hours added to the day are a dubious gain. A mile beyond the

powerline, the night still comes to restore the souls, deep virgin darkness between the embers of the dying fire and the star-scattered vastness of the sky.[7]

Who are we? What does it mean to be a steward of creation? How do we understand ourselves as human beings created for partnership with God's holy spirit in renewing the world? These are questions to be lived into with young people today as we seek to construct ministry in faithful relationship with generations who have gone before and live into a world providing abundance for generations yet to be.

Sustaining practices

For the Reader—

Purchase a field guide for your area, such as the Peterson Field Guide to Eastern Forests or an Audubon guide to the Eastern Seashore. Begin to learn the names of plants, animals, and rocks in your area

For your Youth—

Take your youth group on a hike with cameras, ask them to capture the image that best illustrates joy and love at the moment of creation.

For your Faith Community—

Print and frame what your group decides are the best photos from your hike, present at a worship service that celebrates the joy of Creation and God's love of God's creatures. Find a wall to hang one and rotate the showing of the pictures so that all are seen over the course of a year.

---

7. Kohák, *Embers and* Stars, 29–30.

7

Becoming a Place for Youth

THE PRACTICES OFFERED IN the last chapter aren't going to do much to change our path toward ecological crises, but they might ground the practitioner in this world in ways that open creative responses. Seeing, naming, and learning to live in communion with our world are necessary first steps for the great work before us. I've resisted the pressure to offer tips on how to green your church or youth group; these resources exist and many of them are helpful for challenging a faith community to begin to think about their impact on their world. However, the realization that our generation and the generations following are "coming of age on a finite planet"[1] demand radical changes in our understanding of faith, community, and vocation. I appreciate that many people of faith and their communities are thinking about the environment, but we must dig deeply into our heritage and seek resources for reconstructing community and rethinking faith.

My conversation with Dave remains a significant moment in understanding what is lost in communities that confuses faith and ideology. Dave's decision to become a biologist specializing in wetlands was a decision of integrity necessary for maturing into vocation and to continue to seek meaning. Dave left a Christian ideology providing easy answers, simplistic constructions of God,

---

1. Revkin, "Climate, 'Not the Story of Our Time.'"

and boundaries drawn by a rigid community. In our conversation, I attempted to articulate my deepest commitments in dialogue with a gracious skeptic and found myself completely unprepared. My shallow responses only made sense within the bubble Dave had left, and I was leaving.

My unexamined faith was exposed in this conversation and I saw that it had been damaging to young people when I offered it as a youth minister. Until then, my practice in youth ministry relied on protecting my own unexamined beliefs—felt deeply and passionately—and restating them as primary truth. The world and God had to be as I so firmly believed them to be or . . . well, I did everything I could to avoid completing that sentence.

I fear this is a default practice for many churches and youth ministries. We know something to have been true (for ourselves, for our community, for our particular time). We insist on that understanding until it becomes a bias excluding all other ways of understanding faith. For many young people, this is the community they are leaving. It is a church blind to the deep needs of the world for hope, faith, and love, while striving to protect beliefs that carried it through an imagined past. These churches rather than living as communities of faithful change, become dying communities committed to rigid interpretations of truth. Churches should seek to become communities that engage the world, communities desiring God's love, peace and justice for the world.

The first question for any church seeking to be involved in youth and young adult ministry has to be "how might we offer ourselves to the lives of young people?" Unfortunately, the initial question too often is "how might we attract, persuade, control, or capture youth for the future of our institution?"

Youth and/or young adult ministry can be frustrating. Too often we are mindful of the next challenge, the next program, the latest problem brought by pastor, parent or adolescent. Youth ministry framed by our fear, incuriosity, or incompetence can truncate any understanding of the gospel. I proved this observation true in my first stint in youth ministry in the 1970s and 1980s. Primarily unaware of my own anxiety and entanglements, I became a booster of easy, unthinking assent to simplistic, formulaic beliefs.

This faith confuses discipleship with conformity into existing structures and honors silence in the face of hypocrisy. In other words, it supports formation into what Carlene Bauer calls the official soul. Bauer writes:

> It wasn't that I wanted to stop being a Christian. Peace had been promised to us, so I couldn't give up. As Paul had told the Philippians: work out your own salvation. I had to keep on believing that there were more things in heaven and earth than were dreamt of by area congregations, and that I would one day find a congregation that believed this along with me.
>
> Until then, my teenage soul—suspicious of cheerfulness, though still reflexively respectful of authority— would feel increasingly uncomfortable in the presence of the official soul. The official soul, as transmitted through church and Christian paraphernalia, was upbeat, incurious, happy with its lot. It did not have any heroes other than the ones who appeared in the Bible, and it was content to hear the same stories about these people over and over again. It described pain and suffering in such a way that a person might think alcoholism or the loss of a child were no more inconvenient than a tussle with the flu: after it passed, you could stand in front of the congregation on Sunday and testify that it was all better, and God was good. As far as I could tell, that was the only story told by the official soul, and the real and true sadnesses had been excised for a more mellifluous account. Which made it seem as if there were things you couldn't talk about in church, or with people from church—what made you laugh, why you cried at a movie, what made you angry, or what books you read that hadn't been written by C. S. Lewis, A. W. Tozer, or D. L. Moody. Church was supposed to be the most important thing in life, but so much of life was left out, because so much of its trouble was assumed to be conquered. My pastor mentioned Kierkegaard in a sermon only once, and it would be a long time before I discovered that there was a storied Christian who suffered from, and so in some way

sanctioned, depression, rage, sarcasm, and despair—the diseases that took hold in adolescence, for which church offered no cure.[2]

I was fortunate. I had mentors suspicious of the official soul and comfortable with adolescent despair. My first youth leader, Mac Browning, had a strong sense of what he was calling me toward when he asked me to join him in ministry. It was an appropriate request for a teenage boy and opened a path that neither of us imagined. He asked me to step out of what I knew as true and embrace possibilities I couldn't conceive. This is a gift that has been given to me many times and one I hope to offer to young people, seminary students, and others.

The official soul builds a Christian bubble in order to diminish its encounter with the deep pain of the world. Young people should be trusted to participate in conversations that embrace all of life, not just life as defined by the official soul. Churches must be a place where young people and adults engage in difficult conversations. These conversations are critical. They are essential to our learning to be in solidarity with our fellow creatures and to relearn how to engage with delight our place as partners responsible for Creation's thriving.

Each generation is responsible for faithfully interpreting the wisdom of generations that have gone before and opening faith to the questions of generations that follow. Youth and young adults are leaving churches as they encounter rigidity, fear, and unthinking faith inside our faith communities. We stand with generations who have cultivated faithful change for their time and place when we engage in conversations about faith, theology, ecology, and our place in the world. We find allies and/or antagonists in sermons, doctrines, liturgies, prayers, theological writings, and other resources from our shared history.

In *Journey to the Common Good*, Walter Brueggemann asserts that the church is to be a place for hope and accountability through enacting the journey of renewal. The prophets reveal that the mission of God's people is to "move from scarcity through abundance

2. Bauer, *Not That Kind of Girl*, 41–42.

into neighborliness."[3] Brueggemann finds that the prophets hold the people of God to a higher standard of witness and mission for the life of the world.

> That journey from anxious scarcity through miraculous abundance to a neighborly common good has been particularly trusted to the church and its allies. I take 'Church' here to refer to the institutional church, but I mean it not as a package of truth and control, but as a liturgical interpretive offer to reimagine our world differently. When the church only echoes the world's kingdom of scarcity, then it has failed in its vocation. But the faithful church keeps at the task of living out a journey that points to the common good.[4]

It's not that the church is failing young people, it is that it is failing to live into its vocation as church. Carlene Bauer's desire for a church that lives into the texts it quotes and preaches, rather than the stultifying corporate soul, is a desire for a church that resists conforming into one more institution of anxious scarcity. Dave's decision to leave his Christian tradition rose from the need to seek the truth about the world, and from finding the medieval mindset prescribed for faith to be inadequate.

Jeremiah and Isaiah offer a prophetic (poetic) structure for the church's alternative vision for its vocation. Liturgies become reminders that the church is the community called to witness to God's sustaining love (hesed), God's justice (mispat) and God's vision for righteousness (sedaqah).[5] The Eucharist is the enactment of abundance that opens the church into the long-term practices of neighborliness at the core of their vocation. Liturgy becomes a consistent invitation to nurture life and live through abundance offering the possibility of life-giving community for young people and the world. Brueggemann opens these three grounding aspects of biblical faith:

---

3. Brueggemann, *Journey to the Common Good*, 31.

4. Ibid., 32.

5. Ibid., 62–63.

Steadfast love (*hesed*) is to stand in solidarity, to honor commitments, to be reliable toward all partners.

Justice (*mispat*) in the Old Testament concerns distribution in order to make sure that all members of the community have access to resources and goods for the sake of a viable life of dignity. In covenantal tradition the particular subject of YHWH's justice is the triad 'widow, orphan, immigrant,' those without leverage or muscle to sustain their own legitimate place in society.

Righteousness (*sedaqah*) concerns active intervention in social affairs, taking an initiative to intervene effectively in order to rehabilitate society, to respond to social grievance, and to correct every humanity-diminishing activity.[6]

Jeremiah, prophet/poet, calls God's people to embody these virtues for the life of all, and in opposition to empire and the forces of domination and acquisition. Isaiah proclaims God's steadfast love as a foundation of justice and righteousness for confronting loss, entering grief, living through despair, and renewing hope. The cultivation of our common good arises from the church's entering into the reality of our time. We live in the midst of empire. Our political and economic structures reward the 'wisdom' of those who wield power at the expense of the widow, orphan, and stranger.

However, Brueggemann is clear that there is also shadow in these narratives, an alternative understanding of religious life and God's desire for the world. This counternarrative "resists the neighbor question, because the draw back into the fearful anxious world of Pharaoh is enormously compelling for almost all of us. Our memory fades, and we imagine the security that Pharaoh's system offered and yearn for an imagined wellbeing back there."[7] This shadow church is the church young people are fleeing, it's the church seeking to maintain the corporate soul that Carlene Bauer found so deadly to her continuing in faith. It's the church that maintains a medieval mindset instead of engaging new questions such as how to live faithfully in our ecological crisis, how to be in honest conversation with science, how to be neighbors with people of other faiths.

6. Ibid.
7. Ibid., 44.

Religious communities locating their identity in purity and power with no regard to resources allocated for the life and dignity of all, are seeking their security in this counternarrative. The shadow church is the church of political access, moral judgments, and economic anxiety.[8] It is the church only for those who have resources in the midst of scarcity rather than equity for all as we seek to live in God's abundance. It is a church seeking to avoid our corporate and individual anxiety by surrendering to empire rather than risking neighborliness, justice, and generosity.

With very little imagination, we can extend these competing visions of our life together outside of the church and into our political, economic, and even ecological commitments. Institutions can try to blame outside attacks, but the rot is at our core. The shadow church fears curiosity, passion, and intellectual integrity. We should be supporting young people as they escape from this shadow faith and then follow them out the door, remaining in solidarity as we all seek to live into God's love and justice. This is one of the challenges to the contemporary church of an ecological hermeneutic; can the community be a place where young people thrive rather than merely survive?

The renewal of communal vocation begins in confession and lament, just as liturgies of renewal begin in confession and lament. Our grief and despair find fertile ground as our confession and lament open our faith communities to the poetry and practice of hope. As faith communities seek partners to work for the thriving of all in their parish and the world, they enter into their practice of vocation and open the possibility of vocation for young people. A church that faithfully engages the ideas and visions of generations who have gone before opens faith for generations yet to come by offering a foundation for new possibilities and ways of making meaning. Churches might discover partners as they encounter their own grief and despair through loss, but the vocation of the faith community is found in the poetic/prophetic visions of hope generated as we live into God's love, justice, and righteousness.

8. Ibid., 45.

Carlene Bauer left a church that avoided living into its vocation. She fled the corporate soul and spoke of the Danish philosopher/theologian Kierkegaard as a possible companion for young people in their "depression, rage, sarcasm and despair."[9] But it isn't just the Dane's angst that could appeal to young people, it's also his desire to reveal, provoke, challenge, and call the Christian church to integrity. Kierkegaard sought to strip away the political, economic, cultural, and religious entanglements that allowed his fellow Danes to think of themselves as exemplars of Christianity while avoiding the challenges inherent in living the Gospel.

Clemens Sedmak's model for constructing local theologies begins with the assertion that "(T)heology is an invitation to wake up: to be mindful and attentive."[10] He concludes this wonderful reflection on learning the practice of "little theologies" by reminding the reader that "(d)oing theology entails cultivating the art of hope"[11] and that "(t)heology is the expression of the hope that a few people can make a difference. Theology cultivates the art of hoping."[12] This is truly the "space between" for engaging in ecological theological reflection with young people. It begins through becoming aware, mindful, of the great challenges facing the thriving of life. It is the cultivation of hope, the art of hoping, in the midst of structures, systems and institutions that acquire and maintain power and wealth at the expense of God's desire for God's people to live into the abundance of God's world. Theological reflection remains in the contexts of pain, suffering and death holding out hope and vision for God's *sedeqah, mispat* and *hesed.*

Douglas John Hall spoke of the practice of theology as an integral part of congregational life.

> Theology is what happens, or may happen, when a human being or community lives between God's story of the world, as it is testified to in scripture and tradition, and the world's own story of itself, as it is being told,

9. Bauer, *Not That Kind of Girl*, 42.

10. Sedmak, *Doing Local Theology*, 1.

11. Ibid., 158.

12. Ibid., 159.

explicitly and implicitly, in that particular time and place—that context. It has been the universal testimony of theologians from Paul to Pannenberg, as it was the universal testimony of the prophets of Israel, that there is an ongoing discontinuity, indeed a primal incompatibility, between these two stories—no matter what the character of the world's story in this or that context.[13]

Hall pays particular attention to the orientation to truth at the core of thinking theologically. The prophetic practice found in Brueggemann's invitation to live into God's vision for human thriving in community is an essential element in this truth. The desire to live into stewardship of God's creation for the thriving of all life is another aspect of living this truth. Hall reminds us that theological thinking enlivening the prophetic witness of the church, and of young people, is at best controversial and more often a threat to the comfort, security, and unthinking serenity congregations seek instead of living into their vocation. In cultivating the passion of young people, we have to remain aware we are asking them to step into places that the church will celebrate until required to consider their own commitments and the possibility of change.

Hall continues:

And this, too, is why the churches, with rare exceptions, have had in the past so little enthusiasm for theology. Theology makes you think; it makes you think difficult and uncomfortable thoughts; and it pushes you into relationships and actions that you would likely rather avoid. The notorious anti-intellectualism of most Christian denominations in Canada and the USA is in large measure, I think, a defense mechanism. Most churchfolk want comfort, security, serenity—not truth. And they would rather have a predictable (even a mind-numbing) kind of familiar 'spirituality' than theologically-perceptive sermons and prayers that start the mind ticking and keep insisting that there is another whole way of going about the business of living.[14]

13. Hall, "What is Theology?"
14. Ibid.

The space between the comfort of the church and the passion of young people is the space for pastors to partner with youth as theologians. Young people are already actively practicing theology—they live between worlds and are eager to live into the questions and narratives of faith in relationship to their world. Pastors have the opportunity to engage with young people in exploring the possibilities of theology for deepening faith. Youth/young adult ministers and congregational pastors have the opportunity to reflectively teach and learn with young people and construct lifelong faith viable outside the Christian bubble.

The space between the life of the contemporary North American church and God's steadfast love, justice for those without power, and call for righteousness, is a critical place for theological reflection. We are coming to a time in our history where our appetites far exceed our resources. Honest theological reflection with young people opens the church to being a resilient community challenging the narratives of scarcity. This space is best engaged through an ecological hermeneutic. Young people are waiting to engage big questions about ecology, sustainability, and resilience in their faith communities.

These questions might include: How do we respond faithfully in the midst of all our wealth to the call of Christ? Who are we as a people in a time of war? How do we as a community live in relationship to our land, our watershed? Who are our partners in becoming a community of hospitality for all God's creatures? These questions need to be explored in all our churches through safe, uncomfortable conversations calling the community to greater obedience.

If Candler's Youth Theological Institute, Lancaster Theological Seminary's Leadership Now, and other Lilly funded youth programs have any legacy, it is in opening theological thinking and lifelong faith practices for engagement and critique by adolescents. This commitment requires cultivating a community of older adults, young adults, and youth to engage in theological thinking and faith practices together. I appreciate the time I had with YTI and Leadership Now participating in these communities of practice and inquiry. However, the church could construct these spaces for continuing reflection much better than a summer youth program. Sadly, few choose to.

[handwritten margin note: Suspicious mention of Lilly funding w/ sponsors gift]

Years after my time in leadership, YTI and Leadership Now remain models for how adults and young people can join together to engage theology as poetic, artistic, public practice.

YTI has consistently understood its mission to be the cultivation of public theologians by engaging young people through practices engaging big questions through theological reflection. In these practices, young people would encounter contemporary and historical theological geniuses.[15] High school students and adults read together, unpacking the theologians' commitments to speak truth in their time. Our theological engagement would lead us to engage the big questions of our time such as, where do you see evil existing today? How do we call for peace when everyone is speaking of the necessity of war? How do science and faith describe the world? Are their views incompatible? Complementary? Where are the places of deep longing in our world? Where are places in need of healing? How do you intend to live your life as a person of faith seeking to make a difference in this world?

YTI, Leadership Now and other Lilly funded youth programs shaped understandings of youth ministry for all involved. Our role as mentors and teachers was to walk with young people helping them to cultivate practices for lifelong faith. Our hope was to open space for young people to explore their desire for God and love for the world. Ethel Johnson,[16] our "Wise Woman" at YTI, said every day "God is doing a new thing!" It was a declarative reminder that we were in a sacred community not seeking to define ourselves by all that has gone before, but desiring to come alongside the work of God in this world as authentic disciples living into authentic vocation.

Young people are prophets, theologians, poets, and artists ready to partner with adults to shape, portray, and embody beauty in the midst of a shared life. If our churches could become places for young people to live this, youth could be empowered to claim their

15. Including Augustine, Luther, Aquinas, Barth, Bonhoeffer, Tillich, Rahner, Niehbuhr, McFague, Cone, Ruether, and many others.

16. Ethel Johnson Emeritus Professor of Christian Education from the Methodist Theological School in Ohio. At YTI Ethel served as a listening presence for scholars and a necessary voice of grace for staff. Her entire life is an example of living fully in vocation in all times and places.

nature as creators of beauty. Take your young people out, listen to a poet in an evocative place, find the truth of your presence in the place you love.[17]

When I served as the Director of Leadership Now, we sought to equip young people to be catalysts for shifting the culture of their churches. Leadership Now has a different rhythm than YTI. We had weekend retreats, a week-long summer leadership academy and a summer global experience available for students the year after their summer academy. Our commitment to worship as the center of spiritual formation was true to the Evangelical and Reformed roots of Lancaster Theological Seminary. In 2003 we took students to Taize, France and Geneva, Switzerland for deeper exploration of worship, prayer, and other faith practices. Students were challenged to begin to think of themselves as full participants in the formation and practice of their faith.

We went to France knowing a few Taize choruses, thinking that we understood all that Taize was about. We soon discovered our relative cluelessness about the larger rhythm of prayer, worship, work, silence, communion, and seeking justice governing the gathered community.

After our Taize retreat week, we were exhausted and exhilarated as we settled in for a few days in Switzerland. There our rhythm changed to morning Bible study with a scholar at the World Council of Churches and afternoons wandering the streets of Geneva.

One afternoon we toured the archeological site under the Cathedral of Saint Pierre in Geneva. Under the cathedral with audio guides tilted to our ears, we began to hear about a larger history of worship in this one particular place. Underneath the cathedral, archeologists have uncovered the remains of two fourth-century Christian shrines (one with a working baptismal basin, water still flowing), the foundations of three different churches from three different eras, as well as parts of a mosaic floor from a Roman home.

We walked through a space that generations had shaped to live out their faith. The shrines and churches built in the over 1500

17. If copyright laws were less restrictive, I would quote from Mary Oliver here. Perhaps from "In Blackwater Woods" found in Oliver, *American Primitive*, 82.

years of worship at this site demonstrate the fluidity and diversity of worship in the Christian church. The earliest worship space was built around the baptismal basin. The foundation of a later church was built in the cruciform shape with the space for the Eucharist moving to a place of prominence, while the still functioning baptismal basin was set off to the side. In the twelfth century a large stage area became the focal point as liturgical plays became central to worship. Above the archeological dig sits St. Pierre cathedral. John Calvin preached in this church from 1534–1560. There are still a few windows that show it was first a Catholic worship space, but the walls are white, the pews hard and the only icon is Calvin's Bible.

All of the students on the trip had participated in the Leadership Now summer academy the previous year through a course at Lancaster Theological Seminary with a worship professor. She offered an introduction to liturgical practice, opening questions about who, where and how we worship. The course included a field trip to the Episcopal cathedral in Philadelphia, Pennsylvania.[18] On that visit, we entered a worship space without pews, where the congregation moved from a reading/preaching space to the baptismal font to a third place for the Eucharist. The baptismal font's water constantly flowed with an art piece suspended above it, dedicated to the souls lost in the twin towers terror incident. The space before the ambo was set with facing rows of chairs for congregants to respond to the Word read and proclaimed. At the rear of the sanctuary, in front of the Bishop's chair, was a circle for the Eucharist. The space and the congregation's movement through it called all to participate fully in worship, sparking all of our imaginations about reshaping worship in our home communities. We understood the truth of Michael Warren's proclamation that, "the Eucharist is the sacrament anchoring adolescent faith and offering a bridge to adult faith."[19]

Churches desiring to take on ecology as a core of their mission don't need to begin with a green to-do list. Their first priority is to become a community worthy of the trust of young people. The congregation must cultivate a community of faithful change in

18. http://www.philadelphiacathedral.org/
19. Mahan, et al., *Youth Discipleship*, 42.

conversation with generations who have lived before and in service to generations who will follow. We don't have time for the delusion that we will somehow save the world by becoming ecologically aware, the period for easy answers is long gone. We need to cultivate resilient communities seeking health for the earth and all creatures. In these communities, young people will be nurtured as prophets, theologians, poets, and artists partnering with adults to shape, portray, and embody beauty in the midst of our shared world. When our churches become places for young people to thrive, they open space in which youth claim their nature as creators of beauty and stewards of abundance.

There are churches that do this. I know of places in Central Ohio, Eastern Pennsylvania, North Carolina, Canada, and scattered through the rest of the world. A few have had students involved with the Lilly youth programs, many others have come to their commitments in other ways. These are churches that have done the hard work to make their community a safe place for big questions. They look very different, but they tend to be open to a variety of worship styles, welcome diversity, and are committed to honest dialogue as a foundation for faith in community. These communities write their liturgies through their life together.

A few years earlier, I stood on a beach on Sapelo Island with eleven young adults and an Episcopal priest. Each of us had brought something to the moment of worship, a prayer, a confession, a song, or a poem. Our toes dug down into the sand at sunrise as we offered our call to worship.

> Lord you are the one who calls us to this place, we ask that you bless our gathering as you have blessed our work together discovering your imprint in your creatures and in your creation.
>
> Help us to remember you as the author of all life as we move from this island back to the contexts where we can fool ourselves into thinking we make our own places, our own contexts, forgetting you called all that we love into being.
>
> Help us to remember you this morning at the dawning of this new day. Make today a reminder of your creative

renewal of each day, the promise of new creation, the hope of renewed partnership.

Call life into healing, into wholeness and into hope for the thriving of all your creatures in harmony with creation.[20]

Sustaining practices

For the Reader—

Take a day or weekend for recovery and renewal in vocation. Take time to think about where you are finding hope in your work with young people. Take time to think about where you are caught in despair.

For your Youth—

Ask your young people where there voices are welcomed in the life of the congregation? Where are they silenced? Where are they absent and never missed?

For your Faith Community—

Ask the same three questions of the pastor and a group of adults of your choosing. Begin to rethink how you might become a community of *sedeqah, mispat,* and *hesed* in light of the answers given and the desires expressed.

20. A student prayer reconstructed from field notes and memory.

8

Cultivating Wild Hope

THIS HAS BEEN A heartbreaking spring and summer for anyone who's seeking a sustainable world. The first half of 2012 saw thousands of record high temperatures set for their respective days and a number of cities set all time temperature records. Wildfires have run through the American west as record rainfall events have occurred in Minnesota and Florida. Over 50 percent of the continental United States is currently experiencing some level of drought according to the National Drought Mitigation Center at the University of Nebraska.[1] Early scientific reports are connecting the weather, drought, fire, crop stresses, and additional ecological challenges as evidence of climate change. We are beginning to see the challenges our consumption has created for the world.

On July 8, 2012, Robert Jensen preached a sermon, "Hope is for the Lazy: The Challenge of Our Dead World" at St. Andrews Presbyterian Church in Austin, TX.[2] I came across the audio and text a couple of days later. In this sermon Jensen challenges the congregation to face all the truth of our current ecological reality, not just the truth they believe they can bear. We have entered a time where the peddlers of hope, the optimists, are guilty of the sin of sloth. Easy solutions, easy answers to complex problems, easy hope

1. National Drought Mitigation Center, September 30, 2012.
2. Jensen, "Hope is for the Lazy."

85

keeps us all from facing the full truth of the world we've created. Jensen preaches,

> our world is not broken, it is dead. We are alive, if we choose to be, but the hierarchical systems of exploitation that structure the world in which we live—patriarchy, capitalism, nationalism, white supremacy, and the industrial model—all are dead. It's not just that they cannot be reformed, but that they cannot, and should not, be revived. The death-worship at the heart of those ideologies is exhausting us and the world, and the systems are running down. That means we have to create new systems, and in that monumental task, the odds are against us. What we need is not naïve hope but whatever it is that lies beyond naiveté, beyond hope.[3]

Jensen calls on Wendell Berry, Rabbi Abraham Heschel, and James Baldwin as prophets calling the people to a different way of life. Heschel speaks the truth that though "few are guilty, we are all responsible" in our participation in the human propensity for desecration.[4] In our complicity we fall into the trap of either religious or technological fundamentalism, we believe that one of these will create the magic to save us from the consequences of our exploitation of the world. We have to challenge the very systems in which we have all found our comfort. Jensen is adamant—"Denying reality is not the basis for a winning strategy."[5] I agree that the stakes are too high to do anything but face every aspect of the truth. In our discernment, our practices, and our desire to live into our vocation to join with God for the healing of the world, we have to face the truth about supporting the systems that have created our crisis in the first place. The June 7 issue of *Nature* published a peer-reviewed article authored by twenty-two scientists[6] who found that the earth may be reaching a tipping point similar to that found prior to

---

3. Ibid.
4. Ibid. Jensen quotes Heschel from *The Prophets*.
5. Ibid.
6. Evolutionary biologists, paleontologists, geologists, biophysicists, etc.

earlier extinction events in the geological record.[7] Jensen refers to this scientific paper along with others as he lays out how our culture of death has pushed from exploiting the planet to threatening the systems that sustain life.

Jensen ends his sermon with a call to live toward hope beyond the easy hope of technological or theological optimism. This hope beyond hope echoes the hope of exile. It is the community that faces an uncertain future and lives into grief and joy equally. Jensen proclaims,

> There is a lot riding on whether we have the courage and the strength to accept that danger, joyfully. Don't take my harsh assessment, and the grief that must accompany it, to be a rejection of joy. The two, grief and joy, are not mutually exclusive but, in fact, rely on each other, and define the human condition. As Berry puts it, we live on 'the human estate of grief and joy.'[8] The balancing of the two is the beginning of a hope beyond hope, the willingness not only to embrace that danger but to find joy in it. Our world is dead, but we are alive."[9]

Facing the hard truths about reaching our planetary limits can open deep grief. We begin to perceive the possibility that our children and the generations who will follow will have fewer resources available for their thriving. If we believe that greed and comfort are the reason for our work, then we can get lost in counting things lost. However, faith traditions and their gathered communities speak of a different way to live in relationship. Thomas Berry calls this the core of our great work, to understand that the universe is a communion of subjects rather than a collection of objects. This is our great work, to reimagine life in a culture that has faced the limits of resources and begin to live within the systems that sustain life rather than engineering new ways to exploit them.

7. Barnosky, "Approaching a Shift in Earth's Biosphere."

8. Jensen cites Wendell Berry in transcript: Wendell Berry, The Unsettling of America: Culture and Agriculture, 3rd ed. (San Francisco: Sierra Club, 1996), 106.

9. Jensen, "Hope is for the Lazy."

The contemporary church's vocation begins in lament, just as our liturgies begin in confession and lament. The practices of seeing and listening allow us to begin to see the problems we are inflicting on our local ecologies. Our grief and despair will open fertile ground as our confession and lament open to the poetry and practice of hope. As faith communities seek partners to work for the thriving of all in their parish and the world, they enter into their practice of vocation and open the possibility of vocation for their young people. This is the faithful engagement with generations who have gone before and the opening of faith for generations yet to come that is the foundation for sustaining stewardship. We might discover our partners as we encounter our own grief and despair as the losses are revealed, but the vocation of the faith community is found in the poetic/prophetic visions of hope written as we live into God's love, justice, and righteousness.

There is both grief and joy as we enter into communion. The recognition of death and loss along with the practice of hope in re-newed relationship with holy mystery. Robert Jensen concludes his sermon with one of Wendell Berry's Sabbath poems, but another of Wendell Berry's poems came to my mind, "The Peace of the Wild Things."[10]

HOPE AGAINST HOPE

Reducing waste, recycling, composting, and any number of other green practices are important elements in a group's engagement with our ecological reality, but to understand them as offering any long term hope is foolish. We have to fundamentally change who we are in relationship to our use of resources. We have to understand the consequences of our exploitation of fossil fuels and seek to limit our production of CO_2 and other greenhouse gases. We have to understand how our food is produced and become communities who build soils and raise our food. We have to realize that our impact is so grossly out of proportion to other species, we have damaged the oceans, changed our world's atmosphere. Most importantly, we

10. Berry, *Collected Poems*, 69.

have to realize that there is no separate place called the environment; there is only our home and we are killing our home.

Perhaps I'm overly attached to a particular community on a South Georgia island that gathered together several years ago. I've led similar retreats or courses since and could mine a few of those for illustrative stories, but I am repeatedly drawn back to these people, this place, and our time together because we were able, for a short time, to tell each other the truth as best we could see it.

After twelve miles of paddling the day before, after exploring and seining salt marsh and coastal waters, after struggling to learn a myriad of biotic creatures in geologic and biotic context, we sat under the night sky on Sapelo Island and began our theological discussion. We began with a poem to frame our reflection.[11] Earlier we'd read a short article by Sallie McFague, "Imaging a Theology of Nature: The World as God's Body," pushing us to think of our reflections in ecological theology as beginning with a reflection on bodies. The twelve students sat back for a few minutes at the completion of the poem.

I asked, "It was a full day, what connections are people making between our day, the readings, and who we might be called to be in this world?"

After some initial easy responses from several folks around the circle about 'thinking ecologically' and trying to be better at recycling and/or eating local, Mike said, "I heard the phrase, 'your soft body' and heard it saying that the body was a good thing."

"Yeah, it was 'You don't have to be good,'" Colleen added.

Another voice from the dark circle: "I definitely understand the idea of a soft body, anyone sore?"

"I'm sore but I'm sore not from crawling on my knees asking for repentance but because I worked to get my body to this island," Terence, an athletic young man who found the balance of the kayak beyond his ability to muscle or reason with. After a few moments of laughter, Jen remarked "Do you feel the breeze, can you smell the marsh, this is the first time I can remember thinking of my body in a place, my body in the 'family of things.'"

---

11. "Wild Geese" found in Oliver, *New and Selected Poems*, 110.

The discussion went on as we talked about the rhythm of bodies, of the salt marsh, of the life we'd discovered, and the rhythms of waves, tides and winds. We began to parse our existence as creatures connected in "the family of things." We discussed who we were in relationship with our contexts and the relationship of mind and body within ourselves. We understood these relationships by appropriating the metaphors of the context we were studying. Our discussion became a reflection on the rhythm of the sun, moon, tides and creation.

We turned back to Sallie McFague and remained lively for an hour or so after our scheduled ending time. We talked through our relationships as we thought about McFague's dictum that we love what we know. We explored how to deepen our love of the natural world as we sought to deepen our spiritual awareness of it in the same ways we strengthen our love of God and love of others.[12] We discussed the multiple methods of cultivating awareness and participating in a spirituality that celebrates our groundedness in our earthly context for opening us to God and fellow creatures. McFague challenged us to rediscover our love for God, fellow creatures, and the contexts of creation. One struggle in this practice is to resist the tendency to speak disembodied and decontextually of a deep love of God, ourselves, and life in ecological contexts.

We thought about the fragility of our bodies and then began to think of our responsibility to live in community with other bodies, other creatures moved from bodies to responsibility to the importance of porous community. We called each other out when we offered "correct" answers—answers that only sought to make the speaker look smart—and entered into a space of live metaphors, connections, differences, and open disagreement. We became a community of teacher/learners and learner/teachers.

After our discussion slowed, we concluded and started to our tents for the night. From the small point overlooking the salt marsh where we held our discussion, I made my way a hundred yards to the kitchen area and began some final cleanup left from the night's dinner. I heard someone approaching—"Tim"—I turned when I

12. McFague, "Imaging a Theology of Nature," 203.

heard my name and was engulfed in a full deep embrace, filled with a release of emotion. Noelle just held on saying "Thank you, thank you, I really needed this, you don't know how hard it is to have to remain silent in classes at school and also shut down about what you care most about in church. I needed to talk about this and I think I needed to do it in this place with these people. Thank you."[13]

An ecological hermeneutic isn't a new method for youth ministry, it is choosing to understand that our responsibility to walk with young people toward vocation is a call to live within limits. What I'm proposing is that youth ministry, in fact all ministry, must seek to connect our vocation and our communities with our ecological reality and the best of science and theology to help us all make meaning. A few years ago on Sapelo Island, this community sought to read the world around us in relationship to our understanding of faith. In the years since, I've joined with other communities to do the same. If the church is to be a community that can offer a place for making meaning into the next one hundred years, it will have to read the deep needs of the world with stewardship of the earth as the heart of the Gospel. This practice of environmental midrash[14] is essential for living in our new reality, *Eaarth*.[15]

The communal reading of word and world is at the core of faith. In some faith communities, this practice seeks to protect unexamined beliefs against a perceived attack from outside values. In others, it is the practice of seeking justice, love, and abundance both in the Word and in the life of the world. An ecological hermeneutic offers a foundation for the community's midrash challenging optimistic readings of the word and the world. It demands truth telling about the damage human beings have brought through their selfish exploitation of the world's resources.

We begin this practice by honestly assessing our greed and acknowledging that our desire for comfort threatens future generations' abilities to thrive, or possibly even survive. The faith

13. Conversation reconstructed from field notes.

14. In this work, I understand "midrash" to be the close reading of words and world reinterpreting the words in light of the reality observed in the world.

15. McKibben, *Eaarth*. The title of his book offers a small insight into the stark realities of the new earth we have created.

community's honest engagement with our new *Eaarth* is essential for moving beyond the easy optimism that believes either God or new technology will save us, no matter how serious our mess.

Reading the word and world with young people requires that we place our sacred texts in conversation with science, including the knowledge that we live on a planet that is four and a half billion years old and that we are more deeply related to the life around us than our egos have allowed us to admit. We have to engage the best thinking in evolutionary theory and allow it to shake deeply held convictions. God either is, or is not. Our attempts to defend God's existence do not change this in any way. The aim of the Christian life is to live as if God exists, without any guarantee, and live out the Gospel of Jesus Christ so that it might bring forth *mispat, sedaqah*, and *hesed*.

Sustaining practices

For the Reader—

Find Wendell Berry's poem, "The Peace of the Wild Things."[16] Read it three to four times, taking time between readings in silence. Find a place to go and lie down in the midst of the natural world just as the narrator of the poem did. Write your response to the poem.

For your Youth—

Read Berry's poem for your youth and lead them through the same practice detailed above—don't do this unless you've done the practice already and had time to reflect.

For your Faith Community—

Begin to weave poetry into the life of your faith community. Choose a poet such as Wendell Berry, Mary Oliver, Denise Levertov, or Naomi Shihab Nye and begin to weave their words into sermons, education, etc.

16. Berry, *Collected Poems*, 69. Buy this collection, poets need our support. If you love fiction, Berry's *Jayber Crow* is my favorite novel, so buy it also.

9

Virtues for a Hopeful People

MINISTRY WITH AN ECOLOGICAL HERMENEUTIC

WE'RE BACK TO THE earliest questions framing this book, who are we calling young people to be? What types of adults are we asking young people to become in our time of ecological exile? Can we live as communities that seek to steward all creatures and our shared planet through our new reality? Can we partner with all who choose to live toward justice, righteousness, and steadfast love regardless of how they understand faith and holy mystery?

Christian faith communities have rich resources for becoming communities of ethical grace living into vocation. They can become habitats nurturing young people and seek ways to build sustainable systems cultivating abundance of the world seeking abundance for all. Faith communities living into vocation overturn Bacigalupi's dinner table. They embody God's love, justice, and righteousness for widows, orphans, strangers, and all who are pushed to the margins. They seek abundance for all, conserving resources and cultivating resilience. They offer leverage and power for all people to build lives of dignity. This is the vision for ecological youth ministry, faith communities nurturing young people to take their place as stewards building sustainable and resilient communities for generations yet to be born.

An ecological hermeneutic interprets sacred texts and religious commitments through a desire to live into a world of abundance for all. In this, we confront the hard truths about our exploitation of our world, return to our texts and relearn our contexts in order to seek thriving for our fellow creatures. We cultivate community as a source of healing and wholeness, what Brock and Parker imagine as a sustainable community of ethical grace.

The stories framing this work attempt to emphasize the dire circumstances we have created for our world and future generations.[1] Bacigalupi's banquet is a gut punch illustrating the stark contrast between living in a time of cheap energy and unseen impacts versus the lives of generations who follow. This isn't an image to continue to live into, but one that grounds hope in reality beyond the idea that all our problems are to be left to generations following us.

There are practices and virtues that faith communities can contribute as foundations for sustainable community. The challenge is to live into communities worthy of our young people. These practices begin with careful attention to the world around us. I hope this attention sparks curiosity, compassion, and a desire to cultivate ways of living that seek sustainable abundance for all. Our desire to engage our world should bring us to conversations that place our beliefs in dialogue with the best scientific understanding of our world, one example is the day I spent with Dave delineating wetlands.

It's time to leave the head of the banquet table, move down to where we've sent the scraps, ask for forgiveness, and begin to walk with young people to rediscover abundance. This requires one more practice for adults: resisting the urge to lecture young people on the extent of the crisis. There is no possibility of partnership if it begins with shaming or scolding towards purity. We blew it, they know it, and now we go forward together to discover how to make little moves toward renewing the health of our home.

1. This is not a book of techniques or tips for solving our ecological problems. I don't trust those who offer easy solutions for complex problems. We have traveled beyond simple fixes.

Brian Mahan has written a brilliant meditation on spiritual practice as a way of seeing ourselves truthfully and graciously. He writes of practices for opening the possibility to laugh at and disarm our preoccupation with needing to appear better than we are. Such practices become ways to move into the delight Thomas Merton describes in his vision of God laughing in delight at the moment of our creation. Mahan's work, *Forgetting Ourselves on Purpose* should be required reading for anyone seeking to work with young people.[2] Young people you work with will love to help by pointing out all the ways you fall short of who you claim to be. If you enter into this with the right humor, you may just remain a healthy, honest practitioner, rather than burning out in the attempt to become the glittering image of youth ministry presented in much of the popular literature.

This is what spiritual practices are for. They aren't for Christians to construct a holier or purer illusion of themselves by propping up false pieties. Practices are about seeing ourselves and the world truthfully. Prayer and other practices allow us to "understand reality and ourselves as we really are in order to grow and thrive and become the loving people God wants us to be."[3] This was the yearning of the desert monastics of the fourth and fifth centuries as they fled to the silence of the desert seeking God outside the glittering images so easily found in Rome. Celtic monastics a couple of centuries later sought to imitate the practices of the desert in order to be more deeply human in God's world. Practices offer the possibility of seeing clearly.

Mahan's playful engagement with spiritual practices opens the possibility of moving beyond Dorothy Bass's definition of practices as "things Christian people do together over time in response to and in light of God's active presence for the life of the world."[4] Practices still have this character of formation, emphasized in the earliest records of Christian teaching, but should also move us beyond spiritual ambition and ground our lives by centering us in

2. Mahan, *Forgetting Ourselves on Purpose*. Read carefully, relax, and try some of the exercises.

3. Bondi, *In Ordinary Time*, 22.

4. Bass, *Practicing Our Faith*, 5.

reality. In the past twenty years hundreds of books, articles, and reflections have been written seeking the renewal of the church and the faithful in and through practices. Mark Yaconelli, David White, Don Richter, and others have written wonderful books on practices as the core for youth ministry.

Rather than understanding Christian practices as ways to construct a glittering image for others to admire, practices reveal our self-deception, false commitments, and desires. We engage practices in order to reveal our masks and see past our biases, we learn to, or are helped to resist reinforcing our sense of goodness or spiritual superiority.

Henri Nouwen spoke of ministry as "the ongoing attempt to put one's own search for God, with all the moments of pain and joy, despair and hope, at the disposal of those who want to join this search but do not know how."[5] It is a vision of deep companionship for lifelong faith.

Mike Warren, who has written extensively on youth ministry asks, "What are the skills of discipleship appropriate to a self who has moved beyond childhood and how will they be exhibited by a community of discipleship in such a way that the young might wish to imitate them, seeking out those most skilled in these practices as mentors?"[6] Warren calls for an inconvenient ministry with youth as part of an inconvenient church—a church that lives authentically and radically into the call of the gospel to steward the life of our world. Warren understands this church to arise out of three core convictions:

> First, fidelity is at the heart of any gathering in the name of Jesus. Fidelity to what? To the good news Jesus proclaimed to the poor and the captives and to the way of living embodied in Jesus' own life.
>
> Second, as I stressed at the outset, the prototypical assembly of Christians, the Eucharist, also offers guidance for ministry with youth. The Eucharist defines Christian life as double-sided: offering thanks for the Spirit of Jesus present in the assembly and begging forgiveness for not

5. Nouwen, *Creative Ministry*, 14.

6. Mahan et al., *Awakening Youth Discipleship*, 67.

recognizing the face of Jesus in the hungry, the thirsty, the sick, and the imprisoned, in those without shelter or clothing. It is where we name God's goodness, remember what Jesus endured in the name of justice, and ask for help in living the beatitudes. The Eucharist is the gathering suffused with Jesus' imagination. In this way the Eucharist undermines the Entitled Self of consumer capitalism.[7] It establishes a struggle between God's call to be healers in a broken world and our own worst impulses.

The third conviction regarding youth ministry concerns recognizing the dignity of each young person— honoring the often slow movement of ourselves and others toward the full humanization represented by the imagination of Jesus, recognizing the possibilities in each of more fully embodying the gospel. These very possibilities are what encourage us to propose to young people alternative sensibilities or ways of processing everyday experiences and alternative judgments about which things in life are of greater or lesser value.[8]

I see Bacigalupi's banquet as a narrative that opens Warren's vision of a culture of entitled selves sitting at the table of consumer capitalism. As they eat all that is placed before them, the parents don't hold any cruel intentions, they remain unaware of the cost of their greed. The sumptuous meal is more easily swallowed if they call it God's. They might articulate the blessing as arising from their own hard work and their special place in God's big plan—whatever it takes to reinforce their belief in their right to energy and natural resources without limits or any regard for future generations. It's not their fault that they happen to be God's new chosen, living in God's special land, enjoying an exceptional meal for an exceptional people. No harm intended. This isn't cruelty, just the unexamined beliefs of an entitled self. And the most disturbing aspect of the banquet is that there isn't a "them"; there is only "us." We are all sitting at this banquet, eating and drinking deeply, oblivious to our consumption of the needs of generations to come. Well, maybe

7. For more on the entitled self, see Michael Warren, "The Bottom Line of Youth Ministry: Fostering Self-Esteem," *The Living Light.* 53–65.

8. Mahan et al., *Awakening Youth Discipleship*, 59–60.

you're not, but I seem to be, even as I critique the dining habits of others. So push away from the table, grab the kids, and begin practicing new ways to live into created abundance.

FORMING RESILIENT COMMUNITY

Our *kairos* moment calls for a renewed understanding of the Gospel and human responsibility. Communities of ethical grace arise when people seek to practice good news by stewarding abundance for all creatures living now and generations yet to come. One vision of renewal is to reclaim the Christian gospel as a hopeful expression of life in the midst of the cultures of death. We have an opportunity to pursue our vocation as an act of imaginative, bodily, passionate, compassionate, mindful, critical, historical, celebratory engagement of the full life of human "being," reflecting the character of God's delight and God's creative action in the contexts of the world. The rest of this chapter is a series of short reflections on virtues I hope will become central to the practice of ecological ministry in community.

Discernment

Discernment is "the intentional practice by which a community or an individual seeks, recognizes, and intentionally takes part in the activity of God in concrete situations,"[9] as Frank Rogers defines it. Discernment offers space for youth and adults to engage in seeking the action of God in the world. One historical practice of discernment is the Ignatian "examen." The examen is grounded in the habit of ending each day with questions about where grace was witnessed or where grace was absent. Rogers explains that the practice seeks to develop three particular predispositions in order to deepen the individual's ability to perceive the activity of God:

- *A passionate commitment to follow God.* The guidance that we seek is toward the decision that will bring us into the fullest

9. Bass, *Practicing Our Faith*, 107.

possible participation in the work of God in the world.

- *An attitude of indifference toward all other drives and desires.* If we are to align ourselves with God's purposes, we must first detach ourselves from our desires for wealth, prestige, and security.

- *A deep sensitivity to the ways and being of God.* This sensitivity is cultivated through prayer, reading and meditating on the Scriptures, worship, and faithful acts of mercy and justice.[10]

Rogers explains that these predispositions are typically cultivated on thirty-day retreats, a commitment out of the reach of most youth workers and young people, but these virtues can be nurtured through daily practice. If youth workers would just begin by naming these predispositions as virtues to be cultivated as part of their lives with young people, this simple act could open the possibility of a long term practice.

Discernment is another foundational practice for discovering the possibilities for ministry with youth. David White speaks of the four movements of discernment as listening, understanding, dreaming, and acting. In an ecological hermeneutic, these movements inform how faithful young people and adults can discern ways into right relationship with our contexts and fellow creatures. We begin by learning how to listen carefully for our place in the world, naming, observing, and telling the truth about our place in the world. We explore both the word and the world for texts and contexts to deepen our understanding, rereading texts and contexts as calls to responsibility. In addition to sacred texts, we include the observations of ecological scientists, our understanding of our place in geological time, the narrative of evolutionary theory, and additional observations that push against any understanding that might be locked in a pre-modern or medieval worldview. Rather than declaring our culturally constructed beliefs as the only way of understanding the world, we join with young people in discovering new scientific theories and explanations for the life-sustaining systems of our world. Discernment opens us to nurturing life in

10. Ibid., 109.

our shared world and remaining open to hope in the midst of challenges that seem insurmountable, avoiding the luxury of despair.

Discernment requires humility. Those who engage in careful and self-reflective practices of discernment quickly learn to know themselves as people who are always learning. Such discernment resists arrogance and the demands for purity too often found in both religious and environmental activism. Placing discernment at the core of youth ministry reminds us that we must never act out of certainty or the privilege of our own purity, but as people of faith and integrity working toward richer engagement with the deep needs of the world as partners with the vivifying spirit of God. "The question for the church is not whether God is at work in the world, but whether youth ministry will represent a witness for God or whether it will serve forces that distort humanity and creation's completion in the reign of God."[11]

While those engaged in discernment may begin in any of White's movements, I want to challenge the readers of this work to begin through watching, listening, beginning to perceive what is happening in the natural world. Ecological discernment places these practices in the space between the lives of adolescents and God's vision for the goodness of Creation.

Young people and youth workers must engage in listening, dreaming, understanding, and acting as faithful practices in seeking to join with the life of God in the world. White's organic representation of discernment as a core practice of faith is a rich way to frame a community. I've had the opportunity to witness White teaching his model of discernment with youth and adults. Through these practices, young people find their voices, congregations discover a vision for intergenerational ministry, and all are empowered toward hopeful change. When a community identifies its vocation as seeking creative partnership with the Holy Spirit for healing and justice for the world, everyone and everything changes.[12]

11. White, *Practicing Discernment with Youth*, 208–9.

12. In some of the reviews of White's book, critics have detailed all the ways that discernment could never work. These reviews reveal much more about the imagination and practice of the reviewer rather than any substantive critique of White's model for discernment. Young people and adults who participate

Hospitality

"Well there must be limits to hospitality in nature because Tim keeps killing mosquitoes"

"Ha, okay, as I've said all day, anything willing to eat me gets treated with extreme prejudice"

"Still, Snyder seems to be saying everything he has is open to nature and I think that's weird. He keeps his windows open so deer can grab food off his table, that may be hospitality but . . ."

"Yeah, like Sarah says, I'm all for loving nature and everything, but there have to be limits."

"Well, are there limits to our hospitality as we practice it at home, or in this week together?"

"Yes, there have to be, I'm willing to share some stuff, if you need batteries or part of a granola bar, but I'm not sharing everything, I've only got enough clean underwear for the week."

"Alright, what are the limits to hospitality with nature, how do you keep your sense of who you are as a person and remain open to the possibility of meeting and hosting the stranger through the natural world?"

We'd read "The Porous World"[13] by Gary Snyder and it sparked a discussion that lasted well into the night and was picked up the rest of the week. Snyder described the decisions his family made for their cabin home in California's Sierra Nevada Mountains. Snyder writes,

> It comes down to how one thinks about screens, fences, or dogs. These are often used for keeping the wild at bay. ("Keeping the wild at bay" sounds like fending off hawks and bears, but it is more often a matter of holding back carpenter ants and deer mice.) We came to live a permeable, porous life in our house set among the stands of oak and pine. Our buildings are entirely opened up for the long Sierra summer. Mud daubers make their trips back and forth from inside the house to the edge of the pond

attest to the significance of engaging in discernment as a core lifelong faith practice.

13. Snyder, *A Place in Space*, 192–198.

like tireless little cement trucks, and pour their foundations on beams, in cracks, and (if you're not alert) in
rifle-bore holes and backpack fire nozzles. They dribble
little spots of mud as they go. For mosquitoes, which
are never much of a problem, the house is just another
place to enjoy the shade. At night the bats dash around
the rooms, in and out of the open skylights, swoop down
past your cheek and go out an open sliding door. In the
dark of the night the deer can be heard stretching for the
lore leaves of the apple trees, and at dawn the wild tur-
keys are strolling a few yards from the bed.[14]

The passage hit several buttons for all of us. As has already
been established, I am a mosquito swatter and have been known
to be as dangerous to biting flies and other bearers of six legs with
a thirst for my blood. Others in the group were more gracious and
open. A couple of students had a regular practice of spider and
wasp liberation whenever they were found in danger from humans.
We discussed the hygiene problems associated with mice running
through your home. The article became a central part of our week-
long conversation. We quickly moved from "how can they live like
that?" to "what does permeable and porous mean?" whether in relationship to fellow creatures or even just in the formation of human
communities.

What is hospitality? Where do we practice it? And does it make
sense to speak of hospitality as a practice with fellow creatures and
our shared world? If so, what are healthy boundaries? In our faith
communities, what are the limits to hospitality? Can we even speak
of permeability and porosity as aspects of our communities?

Curiosity

We squatted down and watched the little critters dance.

"What are they doing?"

Taylor Schoettle, a local naturalist, responded: "They're doing
what all creatures do, they are performing to attract a mate."

14. Ibid., 193.

"So these females are dancing to attract a mate?"

"These aren't female fiddler crabs, they're males. The male crab digs a den, keeps it clean and then stands in front waving his large claw saying here I am, great housebuilder, keep the place nice and clean, here I am, fine husband and father, come on over ladies and move in with me. I'm the one you want."

We all laughed, made a few jokes and watched. There were thousands of fiddler crabs in this mud flat. The tide was out, the mud was full of furious activity, claws waving, female crabs scuttling about, a few fights between male crabs, with the tide out we were watching a salt marsh soap opera.

"So what do the crabs do? I mean what purpose do they serve? Do they keep the tidal flats clean?" We'd continued our walk around the island at low tide and dancing crabs were everywhere. We'd seen thousands of demonstrations, tens of thousands of male fiddlers madly cleaning their little dens, fighting, and waving their big claw. "I mean, what's their purpose?"

Taylor paused, offered a gracious chuckle, may have said something about theologians and their need for purpose, and said "They're food."

"What?"

"They're food. Their purpose, if you can call it that, is that they are a link in the food chain. They may process some of the detritus of the tidal flat but not enough to make any real difference, the tides wash through this area twice a day and flush the system quite well. The fiddler crabs are eaten, their larva and young are eaten and they provide a food source for several other species. Is this bad news to you?"

It was. Our theological reflection had failed to take into account the depths of nature "red in tooth and claw." We loved the idea of a world that worked in love and grace, and we could engage the idea of God through this sense of grace, but a species who's primary niche was to serve as food for other species pushed us a bit. It was a good push.

Later that day, walking along a path between a salt marsh and a tidal area, Taylor bent down and turned over a leaf of a plant growing beside the path. Under the leaf, near the stem was a piece of white fuzz resembling the fluff that drifts off of cottonwoods. "This white fluff started to show up a few years ago, we think it's a fungus."

Jenny responded, "I saw something like that in Mexico, it's a fungus, they crush it and use it as a dye for cloth."

Taylor and Jenny continued to talk about what they had discovered in two very different places about a white growth under the leaves of plants at the edge of a salt marsh. It was a brief conversation, but one in which everyone was able to learn from the engaged curiosity of two excellent teachers. Taylor in his many years of learning deeply about the island he loved in South Georgia; Jenny as a young woman living into her curiosity, passion, and desire for the health of our world.

Humility

Humility, humus, of the earth, adam of adamah, men and women created in delight. Humility begins as we lay before the mud covered God celebrating her creation. Our response isn't to take glory in our status, but to humbly accept the imprint of the Creator and gratefully embracing our role as the ones who name and care for the world.

Plant a seed, and start cultivating humility. Place a seed in the ground, water it, weed the area around it, in a few weeks cut the flower, shuck the peas, pick the beans, enjoy. You are of this earth, you are mud from mud, blessed, loved. Be reminded that you are meant for this earth, you are a terrestrial creature as you enjoy the harvest.

In the synoptic gospels of Matthew, Mark, and Luke, Jesus retires to (or is driven into) the wilderness for a time of discernment. After forty days alone, praying, fasting, seeking direction or relief, the text brings in a second character, the tempter. In the first movement, the tempter detects Jesus' hunger—not too hard after a forty day fast—and asks, "Why are you hungry? You can turn any of these stones to bread? Why would you choose hunger when you stand in the midst of all this hidden abundance?" Jesus responds, "Human Beings can't live by bread alone." Jesus is then taken to the top of a high place (Luke and Matthew place this element last in their telling). Here the tempter shows him all the cities and wealth of the world. "Take it all, all this could be yours, all you have to do is worship me—you know, give me my due for this great gift." Jesus quotes scripture, "Worship only God and serve only God."

In the third moment of this narrative, Jesus is told to jump off the top of the high point of the temple, and the tempter assures him that there will be many hundreds of angels will save him from crashing to the ground. Jesus replies, "Do not put God to the test."

These are familiar Lenten lectionary texts. There is a practiced way to illuminate these familiar truths. I've been in a number of churches where the object lesson appears to be obvious to the preacher: these are stories that show the faithfulness of Jesus in the midst of temptation, case closed. These brief narratives are understood as distinguishing Jesus' ministry at the beginning, allowing for a space of discernment that opens Jesus and the reader to the possibility of his being the Messiah. However, the behavior of Jesus' followers in contemporary Western society suggests that the Gospel writers must have left something out. If we're honest about how our faithfulness is played out in relationship to the larger world, it's almost as if there is a lost text that should continue these narratives.

As Jesus turns down the temptation to fulfill his hunger by turning stones to bread (seemingly a relatively minor thing) followers in the twenty-first century are unable to skip a meal. Western Christianity is largely a faith of overconsumption and alienation perceiving salvation as a continuation of our special privilege in the sight of God.

Alan Thein Durning is one of many throughout the years who have posted the question, "How Much is Enough?" It's not a question that is often found at the center of the Christian faith, but it is the question faced by Jesus in the first part of this narrative. It is one that is continually arising during his ministry. Jesus is asked about possessions and answers, "Birds have . . . foxes have . . . but the Son of Man has no place . . ." This is not a lament but a representation of the prophetic ministry of Jesus, an unpopular ministry that is often diminished or ignored in a church complicit with empire. How did the message of abundance in scarcity, the idea of enough, become subjugated to the gluttony of empire?

In the second temptation, Jesus stands high looking down on all the possibilities for power, reward, getting what is due to him. The behavior of contemporary Western Christians suggests that the dialogue continues, maybe Jesus said to the tempter, "I'm not going to take on this power that you offer, but don't sweat it too much, soon, very soon, my followers will stand on every high place and claim every aspect of the power you offer and more. We will own all this and more that the hearers of this story could ever imagine. Christians will speak words of freedom, of hope while making sure they have the first fruits of every harvest."

Humility is not an easy word, humility has been imposed by communities and powerful individuals to control young people, especially to control young women. Be humble, be submissive - meaning, "I have power, you are powerless, I use God to maintain my power and your powerlessness." This isn't humility, it's a practice of domination. The paraphrase above is obviously sarcastic, but hopefully not lost in the sarcasm is the actual narrative of scripture. In the texts of temptation, Jesus is pushed to become like God and yet chooses his incarnate position as a human being, as one of God's creatures.

In our culture of easy celebrity, we need the consistent reminder of dirt, mud, the earth itself that we are creatures celebrated by our mud covered God. This isn't the humility forced upon someone by those who have power over them, but the movement into relationship by engaging in the role we have been created for.

Dig a hole, plant the seedling you bought from your local farmer's market in a few months harvest the tomato, enjoy, you are of this earth, you are mud from mud, blessed, loved, letting the sun, air, water and soil to enter your body after you set these movements in motion. You are again reminded, you are meant for this earth, you are a terrestrial creature participating in the systems for life, relax into your vocation as earth's steward and let the juice of the tomato run down your chin.

Gratitude

"What are you thankful for as you reflect on our day here?"

We had been together for a few days and had learned to settle into silence, resting with the question. Mike took in a breath, "I'm grateful for the breeze that came in with this evening's tide as we sit by this marsh."

Umm, we agreed and then went back to silent rest with the question. After a few minutes: "I'm thinking about how Taylor taught us today. He loves this place and we fell in love with it through him. I'm grateful for his passion."

"I'm grateful for having time to listen, to each other, to Taylor, and to all the sounds I don't ever listen to when I'm rushing about at home."

We were fully involved in our evening ritual. Sitting on a small rise above the salt marsh at the edge of our campground, we had enough space to lounge. The breeze kept the bugs down for the evening, a regular occurrence on this particular spot. On our first night, we'd talked about the *examen* and the possibility of thinking about our day and then closing with a prayer. After I introduced the practice, Jennie brought to the conversation her recent reading of "Sleeping with Bread."[15] She told the story that opens the book: "In a refugees camp, during World War II, children who were there sheltered from the war, had difficulty sleeping . . ."

> During the bombing raids of WWII, thousands of children were orphaned and left to starve. The fortunate ones were rescued and placed in refugee camps where they received food and good care. But many of these children could not sleep at night, fearing waking up to find themselves once again homeless and without food. Finally someone hit upon the idea of giving each child a piece of bread to hold at bedtime. Holding their bread, these children could finally sleep in peace. All through the night the bread reminded them, 'Today I ate and I will eat again tomorrow.'[16]

Jennie continued to explain that the Linn's taught the examen through two simple questions, "For what am I most grateful? For what am I least grateful? These questions help us identify moments

15. Linn et al., *Sleeping with Bread*.
16. Ibid., 1.

of consolation and desolation. For centuries, prayerful people have found direction for their day and for their life by identifying these moments."[17] These questions shaped our evening reflections on retreat and continued as we left our retreat with a desire to cultivate gratitude as a primary ecological practice.

Gratitude is an essential virtue for stewardship. Gratitude allows human beings to assume their place as creatures in God's good creation, rather than despots ruling over all creatures as self appointed superiors. As Christians we understand our place in this world to be a gift from God, not a burden to be borne until we're rescued.

BECOMING COMPANIONS

Walking with young people as they learn about themselves and grow into their vocation isn't one more thing on the to-do list, it is the core of ministry. Youth ministers would be better served if they spent much less time worrying about how to do ministry and more time seeking ways to become more fully themselves in relationships with young people. Dori Baker and Joyce Mercer believe that those of us who walk with young people are in a paradoxical position. We undertake a journey of companionship, grounded in "communally situated journeys that young people in some sense must take alone."[18] This journey is supported through faith communities living into their own vocation, but the response to God's call must come from the young people themselves. Those of us seeking to nurture young people in this call through an ecological hermeneutic can seek to cultivate particular virtues as companions on this journey.

Think back to the earliest story shared in this book, the interpretations from a couple of frustrated pastors about why young people were no longer coming to their programs. In a very simple sense, their interpretation could be right. Young people are too busy and their parents don't make them take the time to do what's

17. Ibid., 2.

18. Baker and Mercer, *Lives to Offer*, 175.

right. We could line up with this easy answer, blame young people and their slacker parents, feel good about our rightness in a wrong world, and move on into ministry with those who understand we're about what's really important, even if nobody gets it. Or, we could choose to enact the abundance of God's world gifted for our stewardship, and live out our communal vocation through the ministry of companionship.

If faith communities choose to live into this vision of ministry with young people, they won't be concerned about why young people aren't coming to church, they'll be out living life alongside young people wherever they are engaging life. If faith communities choose to live out their vocation as stewards for God's good creation, they'll find places to invite young people into practices of stewardship. These core practices arise out of and support some virtues. Neighborliness, for example, is the extension of God's abundance to all people, and through an ecological vision, it becomes the cultivation of God's abundance for all creatures as a primary expression of the church's vocation.

Sustaining practices

For the Reader, your Youth, and your Faith Community—

Organize a meal on the day your local farmer's or community market is selling. Set a budget and go with your youth and young adults to the market. Buy everything you need for the community meal at the farmer's market; wash, chop, sauté, bake, and grill the freshest meal you can imagine from the food you just purchased. After cleanup, show *Urban Roots, Renewal, Food, Inc.,* or another food and justice centered documentary and start the discussion about how you want to be a faith community known for their hospitality, cooperation, and abundant healthy meals.

10

Coda

As contemporary prophets—Bill McKibben, James Gustav Speth, James Hansen, and dozens of others—proclaim, we have changed the systems that sustain life for our world. Our lust for comfort, satiated by harnessing the power contained in fossil fuels storing millions of years of sunlight, has brought us to the end of easy energy. It is time to stop promoting to our young people narcissistic illusions of endless wealth and unlimited progress. We have the opportunity to begin to cultivate communities of shared, sustainable abundance. We cannot continue down the path of more, bigger, richer that seemed easily available just a couple of decades ago. We also can't retreat to the false safety of a Christian bubble, judging everyone and everything that pushes against it as outside the love of God.

We've raised the temperature of our planet by 0.8 degrees Celsius and have pumped enough carbon into the atmosphere for another 0.8 degrees Celsius. We are within 0.4 degrees Celsius of the two degree Celsius temperature shift that scientists[1] have identified as the maximum if we want to maintain the conditions for maintaining human civilization.[2] In a July 2012 Rolling Stone article, Bill

1. Several reports at the end of 2012 have begun to speak of 4 degrees C as a more realistic assessment of temperature change considering current levels of consumption and projected growth in fossil fuel use.

2. McKibben, "Global Warming's Terrifying New Math."

McKibben laid the problem out in stark terms. We have almost five times more carbon based fuels in proven reserves than the earth's systems can bear as CO_2 in order to maintain the climate human civilization has known for eleven thousand years.[3]

We are entering into a time where it is absolutely essential that we, as a species, learn to temper our "infinite aspirations" and shift the "explosive trajectory" of our "consumptive appetite."[4] Churches can be places that build community to bridge the divisions keeping our culture from changing our destructive path. They can live into a renewed vision of community seeking vocation as stewards for the thriving of creation. If churches choose to engage the challenges of our time, these communities will become places young people seek for open dialogue concerning deep questions, vocational discovery, sustainable aspirations, and lifelong faith.

Thich Nhat Hanh asks "(C)an we live in a way that helps us see the causes that are present in the effects and the effects that are present in the causes?"[5] In other words, can we live as interdependent creatures aware of our huge potential for healing our world as well as our propensity for destruction? Youth ministry is best served through the desire to grow in maturity alongside young people as wise companions seeking sustainable community for the health of our world. We have the possibility of living more deeply into vocation and cultivating a deeper awareness of how to care for our world. This is a gift we can nurture from an ecological hermeneutic as a ground for ministry.

There are a number of excellent books that have a more optimistic tone than this one, but the changing biosphere requires more than optimism arising from the good work of a few. Others may have picked this text up thinking I might be a partner in frustration and anger, but I'm not sure another polemic would be helpful to anyone. I am not hopeful but I intend to remain constrained by hope. That is to say, I have no time for optimism that delays hard

---

3. Ibid.

4. Revkin, "Climate, 'Not the Story of Our Time.'"

5. Hanh, *Heart of the Buddha's Teaching*, 225.

political and economic choices while allowing the continuing exploitation of our earth for the wealth of a few.

If this were a better medium for communication you could tell me all the things your community is doing to interpret God's vision for a sustainable world. If I were a better writer maybe I could convey passion and invitation without sounding so preachy. I'll work on the latter but until my skills improve and I can overcome the formational problems of academic communication I'll say it direct. This is an invitation to think about offering spiritual formation in a manner that allows the entire community to seek to be a place of hospitality, cooperation and abundance. Will you join me in seeking to live into a sustainable and abundant world?

Resources for Next Steps

Organizations

    Green Faith
        http://greenfaith.org/

    Interfaith Power & Light
        http://interfaithpowerandlight.org/

    Green Seminary Initiative
        http://www.greenseminaries.org

    Eco Justice Ministries
        http://www.eco-justice.org/

    Earth Charter
        http://www.earthcharterinaction.org/content/

    Yale Forum on Religion and Ecology
        http://fore.research.yale.edu/

    Au Sable Institute of Environmental Studies
        http://ausable.org/

Denominational Resources

    National Council of Churches Ecojustice Working Group
        http://nccecojustice.org/

    UCC Environmental Ministries
        http://www.ucc.org/environmental-ministries/

    UMC General Board of Church and Society
        http://www.umc-gbcs.org/

    Episcopal Ecological Network
        http://www.eenonline.org/

    Lutheran Earth-keeping Network
        http://www.webofcreation.org/LENS/synods.html

Unitarian Universalist Ministry for the Earth
http://uuministryforearth.org/

Evangelical Environmental Network
http://creationcare.org

Movies

Renewal
http://www.renewalproject.net/

Urban Roots
http://www.urbanrootsamerica.com/
urbanrootsamerica.com/Home.html

The Last Mountain
http://thelastmountainmovie.com/

also Everything's Cool; Fresh; Dirt: The Movie; Food, Inc;
The Story of Stuff; The Garden; and many others

Books

Bingham, Sally G. *Love God, Heal Earth*. Pittsburgh: St. Lynn's
Press, 2009.

McKibben, Bill. *Eaarth: Making a Life on a Tough New Planet*.
New York: Holt, 2010.

Moseley, Lyndsay. *Holy Ground: A Gathering of Voices for Creation*. San Francisco: Sierra Club, 2008.

Magazines and Blogs

Orion
http://www.orionmagazine.org

Skeptical Science
http://www.skepticalscience.com

Sojourners

> http://sojo.net/magazine

Union of Concerned Scientists

> http://www.ucsusa.org/global_warming/

Yes! Magazine

> http://www.yesmagazine.org

Bibliography

Anglican Church in Aotearoa, New Zealand, and Polynesia. *A New Zealand Prayer Book*. San Francisco: Harper San Francisco, 1997.

Atkinson, Terry, and Guy Claxton, eds. *The Intuitive Practitioner: On the Value of Not Always Knowing What One is Doing*. Philadelphia: Open University Press, 2000.

Ayers, Ed. *God's Last Offer: Negotiating for a Sustainable Future*. New York: Four Walls Eight Windows, 1999.

Baker, Dori Grinenko and Joyce Ann Mercer. *Lives to Offer: Accompanying Youth on Their Vocational Quests*. Cleveland, OH: Pilgrim Press, 2007.

Baker, Peter. "Drought Puts Food at Risk, US Warns." New York Times, July 19, 2012.

Barnosky, A. D., et al. "Approaching a State Shift in Earth/'s Biosphere." *Nature* 486:7401 (2012) 52–58.

Barth, Karl. *Church Dogmatics*. Vol. 2. New York: Harper and Row, 1962

Bass, Dorothy, ed. *Practicing Our Faith: A Way of Life for a Searching People*. San Francisco: Jossey-Bass, 1997.

Bateson, Gregory. *Steps to an Ecology of Mind: Collected Essays in Anthropology, Psychiatry, Evolution, and Epistemology*. Chicago: University of Chicago Press, 1972.

Bedford, Nancy. "Little Moves Against Destructiveness: Theology and the Practice of Discernment." In *Practicing Theology: Beliefs and Practices in Christian Life*, edited by Miroslav Volf, 157–181. Grand Rapids: Eerdmanns, 2002.

Berry, Thomas. *The Dream of the Earth*. San Francisco: Sierra Club, 1988.

Berry, Wendell. *Collected Poems 1957–1982*. New York: North Point, 1987.

———. *What are People For?*. New York: North Point, 1990.

———. *Another Turn of the Crank*. Washington, DC: Counterpoint, 1995.

———. "Conserving Communities." In *The Case against the Global Economy and for a Turn toward the Local*, edited by Jerry Mander and Edward Goldsmith, 407–417. San Francisco: Sierra, 1996.

Blunden, J., et al., eds., "State of the Climate in 2010." *Bulletin of the American Meteorological Society*, 92:6, 1–266. Online: http://www.ncdc.noaa.gov/bams-state-of-the-climate/2010.php.

Bondi, Roberta. *In Ordinary Time: Healing the Wounds of the Heart*. Nashville, TN: Abingdon, 1996.

Bouma-Prediger, Steven. *For the Beauty of the Earth: A Christian Vision for Creation Care.* Grand Rapids, MI: Baker, 2001.

Bowers, Chet A. *Critical Essays on Education, Modernity, and the Recovery of the Ecological Imperative.* New York: Teachers College Press, 1993.

———. *Educating for an Ecologically Sustainable Culture: Rethinking Moral Education, Creativity, Intelligence, and Other Modern Orthodoxies.* New York: Teachers College Press, 1995.

Brock, Rita Nakashima, and Rebecca Ann Parker. *Saving Paradise: How Christianity Traded Love of This World for Crucifixion and Empire.* Boston: Beacon, 2008.

Brookfield, Stephen D. *Becoming a Critically Reflective Teacher.* San Francisco: Jossey-Bass, 1995.

Brookfield, Stephen D., and Stephen Preskill. *Discussion as a Way of Teaching: Tools and Techniques for Democratic Classrooms.* San Francisco: Jossey-Bass, 1999.

Brueggemann, Walter. *Genesis.* Interpretation. Louisville, KY: Westminster John Knox, 1986.

———. *Journey to the Common Good.* Louisville, KY: Westminster John Knox, 2010.

———. "Hope and Imagination." Video Interview at *The Work of the People,* 4min., 19sec. Online: http://www.theworkofthepeople.com/index.php?ct=store.details&pid=V01105. (Accessed June 7, 2012).

Callicott, J. Baird, and Fernando R. J. da Rocha, eds. *Earth Summit Ethics: Toward a Reconstructive Postmodern Philosophy of Environmental Education.* Albany: State University Press of New York, 1996.

Cobb, John B. *Spiritual Bankruptcy: A Prophetic Call to Action.* Nashville, TN: Abingdon, 2010.

Commoner, Barry. "The Closing Circle: Nature, Man, and Technology." In *The Closing Circle: Nature, Man and Technology.* New York: Knopf, 1971.

Daly, Herman E., and Cobb, Jr. John B. *For the Common Good: Redirecting the Economy toward Community, the Environment, and a Sustainable Future.* Boston: Beacon, 1994.

Durning, Alan Thein. *How Much is Enough: The Consumer Society and the Future of the Earth.* New York: Norton, 1992.

Dykstra, Craig. *Growing in the Life of Faith: Education and Christian Practices.* Louisville, KY: Geneva, 1999.

Eisner, Eliot W. *The Educational Imagination: On the Design and Evaluation of School Programs.* New York: MacMillan, 1985.

Finley, James. *Merton's Palace of Nowhere.* South Bend, IN: Ave Maria, 2003.

Foster, Charles R. "Why Don't They Remember?: Reflections on the Future of Congregational Education." In *Forging a Better Religious Education in the Third Millenium,* edited by James Michael Lee, 89–112. Birmingham, AL: Religious Education Press, 2000.

Fowler, James W. *Becoming Adult, Becoming Christian: Adult Development and Christian Faith.* San Francisco: Jossey-Bass, 2000.

———. *Faithful Change: The Personal and Public Challenges of Postmodern Life.* Nashville, Abingdon Press, 1996.

———. *Stages of Faith: The Psychology of Human Development and the Quest for Meaning.* San Francisco: Harper San Francisco, 1981.

Fowler, James W., and Sam Keen. *Life Maps: Conversations on the Journey of Faith.* Edited by Jerome Berryman. Waco, TX: Word, 1978.

Freire, Paulo. *Education for Critical Consciousness.* New York: Continuum, 1998.

———. "Know, Practice, and Teach the Gospels." *Religious Education* 79:4 (1984) 547–548.

———. *Letters to Cristina: Reflections on My Life and Work.* New York: Routledge, 1996.

———. *Pedagogy of Freedom: Ethics, Democracy, and Civic Courage.* New York: Rowman & Littlefield, 1998.

———. *Pedagogy of the Heart.* New York: Continuum, 1998.

———. *Pedagogy of the Oppressed.* New York: Continuum, 1994.

———. *Teachers as Cultural Workers: Letters to Those Who Dare to Teach.* Boulder, CO: Westview, 1998.

———. *The Politics of Education: Culture, Power, and Liberation.* Westport, CT: Bergin & Garvey, 1985.

Freire, Paulo, and Ira Shor. *A Pedagogy for Liberation: Dialogues on Transforming Education.* Westport, CT: Bergin & Garvey, 1987.

Freire, Paulo, and Myles Horton. *We Make This Road by Walking: Conversations on Education and Social Change.* Philadelphia: Temple University Press, 1990.

Fromm, Erich. *The Anatomy of Human Destructiveness.* New York: Holt, 1973.

Gebara, Ivone. *Longing for Running Water: Ecofeminism and Liberation.* Minneapolis, MN: Fortress, 1999.

Gergen, Kenneth. *The Saturated Self: Dilemmas of Identity in Contemporary Life.* New York: Basic Books, 2000.

Gottlieb, Roger S., ed. *This Sacred Earth: Religion, Nature, Environment.* New York: Routledge, 1996.

Greene, Maxine. *The Dialectic of Freedom.* New York: Teachers College Press, 1988.

———. *Releasing the Imagination: Essays on Education, the Arts, and Social Change.* San Francisco: Jossey-Bass Publishers, 1995.

———. "Towards Wide-Awakeness: An Argument for the Arts and Humanities in Education." In *Landscapes of Learning*, 161–167. New York: Teachers College Press, 1978.

Grossman, Cathy Lynn and Stephanie Steinberg. "'Forget Pizza Parties,' Teens Tell Churches." *USA Today* August 11, 2010.

Hall, Douglas John. *Confessing the Faith: Christian Theology in a North American Context.* Minneapolis, MN: Fortress, 1998.

———. *Professing the Faith: Christian Theology in a North American Context.* Minneapolis, MN: Fortress, 1996.

———. *The Stewardship of Life in the Kingdom of Death.* Grand Rapids: Eerdmans, 1985.

———. *Thinking the Faith: Christian Theology in a North American Context.* Minneapolis MN: Fortress, 1991.

———. "What is Theology and Why Does the Church Need It?" September 15, 2003. Ottawa Lay School of Theology. Online: http://web.archive.org /web/20090503144519/http:/www.olst.ca/hall.htm.

Hallie, Philip P. *Lest Innocent Blood Be Shed: The Story of the Village of Le Chambon and How Goodness Happened There.* New York: Harper & Row, 1979.

Hansen, James, et al. *Target Atmospheric CO2: Where Should Humanity Aim?* NASA Goddard Institute for Space Studies, 2008

———. "Why I Must Speak Out About Climate Change." TED video 17min., 51sec. Posted March 2012, Online: http://www.ted.com/talks/jame s_hansen_why_i_must_speak_out_about_climate_change.html

Hessel, Dieter T., ed. *After Nature's Revolt: Eco-Justice and Theology.* Minneapolis, MN: Fortress, 1992.

———. *Theology for Earth Community: A Field Guide.* Minneapolis, MN: Fortress, 1996.

Hirshfield, Jane. *The Lives of the Heart: Poems.* San Francisco: HarperCollins, 1997.

Intergovernmental Panel on Climate Change. *Workshop Report of the Intergovernmental Panel on Climate Change Workshop on Sea Level Rise and Ice Sheet Instabilities.* Edited by T. F. Stocker et al. Bern, Switzerland: University of Bern, 2010. Online: https://www.ipcc-wg1.unibe.ch/ publications/supportingmaterial/SLW_WorkshopReport.pdf

———. *Climate Change 2007: Synthesis Report..* Edited by R. K Pachauri, and A. Reisinger. (November 2007). Online: http://www.ipcc.ch/pdf/assessment-report/ar4/syr/ar4_syr.pdf.

———. "Summary for Policymakers." In *Managing the Risks of Extreme Events and Disasters to Advance Climate Change Adaptation.* Edited by C. B. Field et al., 1–19. Cambridge, UK: Cambridge University Press, 2012.

Isasi-Diaz, Ada Maria. *En la Lucha: Elaborating a Mujerista Theology.* Minneapolis: Fortress, 1993.

Jackson, Wes. *Altars of Unhewn Stone: Science and the Earth.* New York: Farrar, Straus, and Giroux, 1995.

———. *Becoming Native to this Place.* Washington, DC: Counterpoint, 1994.

Jackson, Wes, and William Vitek, eds. *Rooted in the Land: Essays on Community and Place.* New Haven, CT: Yale University Press, 1996.

Jensen, Robert. "Hope is for the Lazy: The Challenge of Our Dead World." (MP3 audio file) Online: http://www.staopen.com/podcast/2012/jensen 7_8_2012.mp3.

Jowit, Juliette. "World's glaciers Continue to Melt at Historic Rates." *The Guardian,* January 25, 2010.

Karl, T. R., et al. "Global Climate Change Impacts in the United States." *US Global Change Research Program (USGCRP)*. Washington, DC: Cambridge University Press. Online at: http://downloads.globalchange. gov/usimpacts/pdfs/climate-impacts-report, 2009.

Kinnaman, David, and Aly Hawkins. *You Lost Me: Why Young Christians Are Leaving Church—and Rethinking Faith*. Grand Rapids: Baker, 2011.

Kinnaman, David, and Gabe Lyons. *Unchristian: What a New Generation Really Thinks About Christianity—and Why It Matters*. Grand Rapids: Baker, 2007.

Kraft, Richard J. and Mitchell Sakofs, eds. *The Theory of Experiential Education*. Boulder, CO: Association of Experiential Education, 1985.

Kosmin, B. A., et al. *American Nones: The Profile of the No Religion Population, A Report Based on the American Religious Identification Survey* 2008. Hartfort, CT: Trinity College, 2009.

Lakoff, George and Mark Johnson. *Philosophy in the Flesh: The Embodied Mind and its Challenge to Western Thought*. New York: Basic Books, 1999.

Lamm, Norman. "Ecology in Jewish Law and Theology." In *Torah of the Earth: Exploring 4,000 Years of Ecology in Jewish Thought*. Vol. 1 of Biblical Israel & Rabbinic Judaism, edited by Arthur Waskow, 103–126. Woodstock, VT: Jewish Lights, 2000.

Leopold, Aldo. *A Sand County Almanac and Sketches Here and There*. New York: Oxford University Press, 1989.

Levertov, Denise. *The Life Around Us: Selected Poems on Nature*. New York: New Directions, 1997.

———. *Sands of the Well*. New York: New Directions, 1998.

McFague, Sallie. *The Body of God: An Ecological Theology*. Minneapolis, MN: Fortress, 1993.

———. "Imagining a Theology of Nature: The World as God's Body." In *Liberating Life: Contemporary Approaches to Ecological Theology*, edited by Charles Birch et al., 201–227. Maryknoll, NY: Orbis, 1990.

———. *Models of God: Theology for an Ecological, Nuclear Age*. Minneapolis, MN: Fortress, 1987.

———. *Super, Natural Christians: How We Should Love Nature*. Minneapolis, MN: Fortress, 1997.

McKibben, Bill. *Eaarth: Making a Life on a Tough New Planet*. New York: Holt, 2010.

———. *The End of Nature*. New York: Doubleday Anchor, 1989.

———. "Why the Energy-Industrial Elite Has It In for the Planet" TomDispatch, February 7, 2012. Online: http://www.tomdispatch.com/archive/175499/.

Midgley, Mary. *Beast and Man: The Roots of Human Nature*. New York: Routledge, 1995.

———. "Consciousness, Fatalism, and Science." In *The Human Person in Science and Theology*, edited by Niels Henrik Gregersen et al., 21–40. Grand Rapids: Eerdmans, 2000.

———. *Science and Poetry*. New York: Routledge, 2001.

Moore, Mary Elizabeth. *Ministering with the Earth*. St. Louis, MO: Chalice, 1998.

National Oceanic and Atmospheric Administration. "Carbon dioxide levels reach milestone at Arctic sites." Online: http://researchmatters.noaa. gov/news/Pages/arcticCO2.aspx

———. "2010 Tied for Warmest Year on Record." Online: http://www.noaanews .noaa.gov/stories2011/20110112_globalstats.html

Nicholson, Sherry Weber. *The Love of Nature and the End of the World: The Unspoken Dimensions of Environmental Concern*. Cambridge: MIT Press, 2002.

Oelschlaeger, Max. *The Idea of Wilderness: From Prehistory to the Age of Ecology*. New Haven, CT: Yale University Press, 1991.

Oliver, Mary. *American Primitive*. New York: Little, Brown, 1978.

———. *New and Selected Poems*. Boston: Beacon, 1992.

———. *West Wind: Poems and Prose Poems*. Boston: Houghton Mifflin, 1997.

Orr, David W. *Ecological Literacy: Education and the Transition to a Postmodern World*. New York: SUNY Press, 1992.

———. *Earth in Mind: On Education, Environment, and the Human Prospect*. Washington, DC: Island, 1994.

Peterson, Anne L. *Being Human: Ethics, Environment, and Our Place in the World*. Berkeley: University of California Press, 2001.

Petty, Michael W. *A Faith that Loves the Earth: The Ecological Theology of Karl Rahner*. New York: University Press of America, 1996.

Rahner, Karl. *Foundations of Christian Faith: An Introduction to the Idea of Christianity*. New York: Crossroads, 1996.

Rahner, Karl, and Geoffrey B. Kelly (ed.). *Karl Rahner: Theologian of the Graced Search for Meaning*. Minneapolis, MN: Fortress, 1992.

Revkin, Andrew C. "'Climate, Not the Story of Our Time.'" *New York Times*. New York Times blogs, December 1, 2008. Online: http://dotearth. blogs.nytimes.com/2008/12/01/climate-not-the-story-of-our-time/?emc=eta1

Rogers, A. D. and D.d'A Laffoley. *International Earth System Expert Workshop on Ocean Stresses and Impacts*. Summary Report, 18pp. IPSO Oxford, 2011. Online: http://www.stateoftheocean.org/pdfs/1906_IPSO-LONG.pdf

Rogers, Frank. "Discernment." In *Practicing Our Faith: A Way for a Searching People*, edited by Dorothy Bass, 105–118. San Francisco: Jossey-Bass, 1997.

Rossing, Barbara R. *The Rapture Exposed: The Message of Hope in the Book of Revelation*. Boulder, CO: Westview, 2004.

Rukeyser, Muriel. *The Life of Poetry*. Ashfield, MA: Paris Press, 1996.

Scalzi, John. *The Big Idea - Paulo Bacigalupi*. Whatever (blog). http://whatever. scalzi.com/2010/05/20/the-big-idea-paolo-bacigalupi-2/ (accessed May 20, 2010).

Schneiderman, Jill S, ed. *The Earth Around Us: Maintaining a Livable Planet*. New York: Freeman, 2000.

Schoettle, Taylor. *A Guide to a Georgia Sea Island: Featuring Jekyll Island with St. Simons and Sapelo Islands.* St. Simons Island, GA: Watermark's, 1996.

Schumacher, E. F. *Small is Beautiful: Economics as if People Mattered.* San Francisco: HarperPerrenial, 1973.

Sedmak, Clemens. *Doing Local Theology: A Guide for Artisans of a New Humanity.* Maryknoll, NY: Orbis, 2002.

Sessions, George, ed. *Deep Ecology for the 21st Century: Readings on the Philosophy and Practice of the New Environmentalism.* Boston: Shambala, 1995.

Seton, Ernest Thompson. *Two Little Savages: Being the adventures of two boys who lived as Indians and what they learned.* Mineola, NY: Dover, 1962.

Shabecoff, Phillip. "Global Warming has Begun." New York Times, June 24, 1988. Online: http://www.nytimes.com/1988/06/24/us/global-warming-has-begun -expert-tells-senate.html

Sideris, Lisa H. "Ecology and the Environment." In *The Blackwell Companion to Science and Christianity*, edited by J. B. Stump and Alan G. Padget, 406–417. Wiley, 2012.

Sittler, Joseph. *The Care of the Earth.* Minneapolis, MN: Fortress, 2004.

Snyder, Gary. *A Place in Space: Ethics, Aesthetics, and Watersheds.* New York: Farrar, Straus, and Giroux, 1990.

———. *Mountains and Rivers without End.* Washington, DC: Counterpoint, 1996.

———. *No Nature: New and Selected Poems.* New York: Pantheon, 1997.

Swimme, Brian, and Thomas Berry. *The Universe Story: From the Primordial Flaring Forth to the Ecozoic Era: A Celebration of the Unfolding of the Cosmos.* San Francisco: HarperSanFrancisco, 1992.

Teal, John, and Mildred Teal. *Life and Death of the Salt Marsh.* New York: Ballantine, 1969.

Tracy, David. *On Naming the Present: Reflections on God, Hermeneutics, and the Church.* Maryknoll, NY: Orbis, 1994.

Tucker, G M. "The Peaceable Kingdom and a Covenant with the Wild Animals." In *God Who Creates: Essays in Honor of W. Sibley Towner*, edited by S. Dean McBride, Jr. and William P. Brown, 215–225. Grand Rapids: Eerdmans, 2000.

Van Matre, Steve. *Earth Education: A New Beginning.* Greenville, WV: The Institute for Earth Education, 1990.

Volf, Miroslav, and Dorothy C. Bass, eds. *Practicing Theology: Beliefs and Practices in Christian Life.* Grand Rapids: Eerdmans, 2002.

Wagoner, David. "Lost." In *The House of Belonging.* By David Whyte. Langley, WA: Many Rivers Press, 1998.

Warren, Michael. "The Bottom Line of Youth Ministry: Fostering Self-Esteem," *The Living Light*, 2000 vol. 35, no. 3, p. 53-65.

Waskow, Arthur. "Earth, Social Justice, and Social Transformation: The Spirals of Sabbatical Release." In vol. 1 of *Torah of the Earth: Exploring 4,000 Years of Ecology in Jewish Thought*, edited by Arthur Waskow, 70–83. Woodstock, VT: Jewish Lights Publishing, 2000.

Bibliography

White, Jr., Lynn. "The Historical Roots of Our Ecologic Crisis." *Science* 35:3767 (March 10, 1967) 1203–1207.

Whitehead, Alfred North. *The Aims of Education and Other Essays*. New York: Free Press, 1929.

Williams, Terry Tempest. *Leap*. New York: Pantheon, 2000.

Wilson, Edward O. *Consilience: The Unity of Knowledge*. New York: Random House, 1999.

Wright, N. T. "Jesus Is Coming—Plant a Tree!" In *The Green Bible*, edited by Michael G Maudlin and Marlene Baer, 72–85. San Francisco: HarperOne, 2008.

Yahgulanaas, Michael Nicoll, et al. *Flight of the Hummingbird: A Parable for the Environment*. Berkeley: Greystone, 2008.